About the Author

After a varied career embracing teaching, public relations, lobbying and business management, Frank Wingate is again teaching and writing.

Growing up in a small village in Hertfordshire, he studied at Oxford and then spent over 20 years in Hong Kong, before returning to London.

Dedication

For my sisters, Sue and Sally, and my brother Geoff, who
all shared in this story.

Frank Wingate

GOODBYE TO THE HORSE VILLAGE

AUSTIN MACAULEY PUBLISHERS™

LONDON • CAMBRIDGE • NEW YORK • SHARJAH

A CIP catalogue record for this title is available from the British Library.

ISBN 9781788231497 (Paperback)
ISBN 9781788231503 (E-Book)
www.austinmacauley.com

First Published (2017)
Austin Macauley Publishers Ltd.
25 Canada Square
Canary Wharf
London
E14 5LQ

Acknowledgements

Reginald Hine, for his authoritative History of Hitchin.
Daphne Rance, for her scholarly history of 19th century
St Ippolyts.

Sally Wingate, for her research into Wingate family history.

Contents

The Cold and the Warmth 13

What's in a Name? 31

World Outside 35

Settlers 53

Arrivals 58

Posh, Common or Normal 69

Church on the Hill 81

Days of the Year 85

Hosting Henry 100

Charlie and Brenda 119

Secret Preacher 132

Inkwells and Jesus 136

Education. Education. Education. 156

Bandits on the Beach 162

Riot and Dissent 175

Alfie Turner 183

Changes 189

Exile 201

Growing up in 1950s Britain

Chapter One
The Cold and the Warmth

On the harsher winter mornings, when we woke up, there would be a layer of ice on the inside of our bedroom window. I would look at it, clutching the bedclothes tight round my neck, and observing my breath frozen in the chill air. But from the neck down my body was well cocooned. Having gone to bed wearing a vest and socks and thick flannel striped pyjamas, tied with a cord at the waist, I was bedecked in two sheets, two thick blankets, a padded eiderdown and a bed cover. It was heavy, but snug.

Waking up itself was a positive process. A cheap but quaint alarm clock sat on my bedside table. A five-inch-high gold-coloured instrument, with transparent sides showing its inner workings, it was topped by a thumb-size ballerina, enclosed in a bell shaped plastic cover. At the chosen time it would tinkle out the well-known musical tune of "Oh what a lovely morning, Oh what a lovely day" while the dainty ballerina performed a stiff pirouette. It never occurred to me as an eleven-year-old that this would have reflected poorly on my image among my peers had it become public knowledge. I found it a gentle and comforting way of regaining consciousness as I met the new day.

Getting up, on the other hand, was a tribulation in winter and to be delayed as long as possible. Our council house had no central heating – that was a luxury few but the wealthy could afford – so the only warmth was generated from the tiny open fireplace in the living room downstairs. But that had to wait until Mum or Dad had laid the paper and wood and ignited the coal that had to be brought in with the coal scuttle from the shed outside.

Necessity had taught me how to confront the challenge of emerging from my protective nest. Next day's clothes had been folded on the bottom of the bed in careful order. On top a shirt, then a sweater. Next, underneath, shorts. Boys wore grey shorts on school days, whatever the weather and, finally, long socks, assuming I hadn't decided to wear them in bed, against my mother's wishes.

This facilitated a well-practised routine. On a count of three, sit up, and before the refrigerated atmosphere of the room could numb me, throw off my pyjama top and hurriedly pull on and button up my shirt. Heave on my sweater over my head. Then leap out of bed and swiftly replace my pyjama trousers with underpants and grey shorts, before putting on socks and shoes.

After this came a reluctant trip to a freezing bathroom, where cold water was splashed over face and hands, remembering Dad's frequent admonition to "wash behind the ears". I never quite understood this insistence, as I didn't see how dirt could get there, but it was made clear that cleanliness in this obscure neck area helped mark us out as distinct from the urchins of the village.

Our house, 56 Waterdell Lane, in the Hertfordshire village of St. Ippolyts, was idyllic. At the end of a row of council houses built in the 1930s, it had three bedrooms, two downstairs rooms, a kitchen and a scullery. Most of our family life took place in the cramped living room and the kitchen. The other ground floor room, however, was the "Front Room" and sacrosanct. My father used it occasionally to do his "papers" – an exercise which flustered and irritated him. But us children – there were three of us by then – were not allowed in except on special occasions.

In the Front Room was exhibited our best furniture and bric-a-brac. On the mantelpiece was my parents' wedding photo. Respectively handsome and beautiful, their hairstyles mimicking the film stars of the 1940s. I had little interest in the Front Room anyway. It was cold and unfriendly and smelt of furniture polish. We weren't supposed to play there. When we were allowed in, at special times like Christmas, or when relatives or VIP guests had to be entertained, we were required to be on our best behaviour.

As a result, the five of us spent most domestic time in the living room in winter, huddled around the fire. Supplementary heating was provided by a paraffin heater, but it smelt of burning oil and we were constantly warned not to touch it. It would not only burn us, but if upset "would cause a fire and burn the whole house down."

The kitchen, where, along with the scullery, my mother spent most of her time, cooking and washing and scrubbing and boiling sheets in the large copper cauldron, was sparse. With a linoleum covered floor and whitewashed walls, it had a large deep sink, next to a gas cooker and oven. The sink served as bath tub as well as dish washer. Many an evening I stood in that large sink, while my mother scraped layers of mud from my knees and legs and washed me in preparation for going to bed. As she washed she would gently scold me for getting myself so dirty, but her soft rebukes did little to deter me, because she couldn't understand that playing football, and being in goal in particular, required heroic diving around, however soggy or wet the ground.

We had no fridge, but a pantry, which was open to the outside by means of an open window, covered by a fine wire mesh, designed to let in the cold, but keep out the bluebottles in the summer.

We were lucky. Number 56 was one of the houses which had both an inside toilet and bathroom, upstairs. Not only that, we had an attached outside toilet as well, next to the coal shed, which meant you could reach it without going outside. This was unlike the council houses across the recreation ground, where Martin Saich lived, which had no bathroom and only one outside toilet. I know this because Martin told me of his determined efforts to use the toilet in daylight, as it was scary going out into the garden to use it on dark wintry evenings. I had also experienced their privy at night, when I had been invited to a party, and it was truly nerve-racking.

As the end of the terrace, our semi-detached number 56 enjoyed a relatively generous garden. In front were two rectangular lawns, about four yards wide and ten yards long, divided by a concrete path running direct from front gate to our front door. Us children were not allowed on the grass, and the front door was rarely used, except for those special visitations which also demanded the opening up of the front room.

To one side of the lawns was a semi-cultivated area, dominated by an ancient, moss-covered greengage tree. It did produce fruit every few years, and my sister and I ate the greengages un-ripened, which normally resulted in indigestion and stomach ache.

At the side of the house lay my favourite area. It had once been a lawn, but only a few sad tufts of grass survived, on account of my requisitioning the area as my private football pitch, tennis court and general play area. Here I spent many happy, intense hours, with my imagination running riot, as I incessantly booted a football against the side of the house, on which I had chalked a goal. Occasionally, my patient mother, understandably demented by the repetitious thumping, came out to tell me to stop, and I did, for a while. But the demands of the cup final, with Luton Town leading Spurs, or the international with England playing Brazil, were too compelling and soon I was back in my own world, dribbling around the base of the old bird bath and crashing a shot into the goal, trapping the rebound and drilling another effort against the wall.

At the back, lay another garden area, which stretched away extensively. It was mainly cultivated with rows of potatoes, cabbage, Brussels sprouts, onions and carrots at the right times of the year. Behind it all, at the rear, a disused chicken shed. About four feet high, three feet wide and six feet long, with a narrow low door one end and a number of small apertures along the sides, no more than a few inches in diameter, the black pitched shack had been requisitioned as a submarine.

In here I would hide away from the world at great depths in the ocean and, invisible, hunt the Tirpitz, or the Bismarck, or the Japanese aircraft carriers of Yamamoto, until my heroic reveries were interrupted by my tiresome sister asking me what I was doing "crawling around in that chicken shit" or my mother called me in for tea.

Our back yard, some 40 yards long, had also served another purpose, besides supplementing our family diet with fresh vegetables. It was, no less, the training ground of a future Olympic champion. Having come third in the North Herts under 11 Long Jump Competition, I had been inspired to greatness, and was convinced, with sufficient training, I could easily improve on the 11 feet 7 inches I had achieved at the meet and one day challenge the best in the world.

However, it was obvious I would need relentless practice and my own long jump pit. Now the garden path at the back ran in a straight line, for about 30 yards, between the vegetable patches from the back door up to an uncultivated patch just before the hawthorn bushes which marked the boundary.

I calculated that thirty yards was just about right for a long jump run-up. Although the cement on the path was cracked and uneven, it would do. I then spent many hours digging out the landing pit at the end of the path. My father wasn't entirely happy with the construction as I had to pile up the extracted earth in an unsightly heap. Neither did he like the idea of me filling my pit with sand, which was my intention. It would, he thought, make a mess and be easily spread over the entire area.

However, not to be daunted, I hit on the idea of wood shavings and he reluctantly agreed to this solution. I found a source fairly easily, for my classmate Peter Dawson was from a farming family, whose land was not far outside the village and he offered me as much as I needed. This meant I had to spend an afternoon playing with him on the farm in return. This was not a bad deal, for I liked Peter, although he wasn't very good at football and his mother only gave us plain bread and butter for tea, without jam or anything, which I found strange.

I then had the logistical problem of getting three large sacks full of wood shavings home, but Mrs Dawson, who, with her cloth cap, dressed and looked like a man, came to the rescue. She drove me home in the Land Rover, with my booty in the back, and so I returned in triumph. The sacks were immediately emptied and I practised non-stop that very evening for two hours before darkness descended on the Olympian scene. My passion for long-jumping didn't last very long, however – perhaps a week – for try as I might I couldn't seem to get beyond 11 feet 7 inches. The dry wood shavings were gradually dispersed by the wind and rain and the pit lay like a shallow empty grave for many months after.

In the winter, playtime in the garden or beyond was short, as the early dusk on chilly evenings drove us into the warmth of home and the living room. Within reach of the glowing coal fire, from which we were protected by the wrought iron fireguard, my sister, brother and I played games, squabbled endlessly, ate and watched TV, under the protective and ever-present guardianship of my mother, who worked constantly on the household, when not caring for our needs. She didn't read to us, or talk to us much, but her permanent background existence, taken entirely for granted, was a constant reassurance that we were safe, loved, and protected from the evils of the world lurking in the village blackness and howling winds outside.

My mother was beautiful. That was not just my opinion, for Mrs Jenkins, my friend David's mum, had told me several times that my mother and father were the most handsome couple in the village and that mum was a "real beauty". Coming from London, she found country life very quiet and dull. She laboured incessantly and dutifully, but was happiest when there was a hint of a party, celebration or amusing company. With her long black hair, shapely figure and flashing white smile, there is little doubt she should have been a film star. But she was here, looking after us and showering us with affection, reprimanding us gently, never losing her temper. She was sometimes lonely, with few friends, or even human contact. She did have Auntie Audrey, who was younger and came to help occasionally, especially after my youngest sister, Sally, was born. But otherwise conversation was restricted to brief gossip in the village store with Mrs Tooley, whose establishment was visited at least once a day to stock up on food and provisions. Mrs Tooley was very old, however, quite grumpy and not at all like a film star.

Mum had not been warmly received by my father's parents, with whom they had lived in another small council house, before being allocated their own. My uncles, however, particularly Uncle Charlie, who was "a bit of a devil with the ladies", liked her and she flirted with them. Uncle Charlie would pat her bottom and say things that made her laugh. "Charlie, you're awful", she would say, but I never understood what he said that was so amusing. Life, for my mother, was a tribulation. She responded to that by acting passively and repressing her own intelligence. "Your mother's an intelligent woman," my father would say to us, "But doesn't use her brains."

I couldn't see why she should "Use her intelligence". She had my sister, me and brother Geoff for company and we took care of her. Our life was fulfilled. We liked having her at home for us.

My father was the stronger character of the two. Raised in the village since he was eleven years old, he loved his community. As a famous local footballer, when I was very young, he was well known in the nearby town of Hitchin, and its surrounding villages. I was always slightly bemused, but proud, that so many people greeted him warmly when we walked hand in hand down Hitchin High Street on weekend shopping trips. They came up and shook his hand and talked of exploits and games that seemed like history to me. "Who's that?" I'd ask, and he would say "Oh, that's Rubber Larman, or Wink Saunders, or Larry Dolan, who was a "Useful left half", or "Just one of the fans".

He was a self-made man. Or, rather, he was made by the Second World War. Having left the village school at fourteen years old, his first job was as a delivery boy for the Co-operative in Hitchin. He would cycle miles and miles around the town and villages of North Hertfordshire on a big-framed bike, with a huge woven basket stacked full of groceries on the front. No gears, just muscle power to push him along. Perhaps that's why he was so athletic.

That would have been his fate, except, when he was twenty-one, in 1939, the war broke out and he was called up to do his duty for King and Country. Fortunately for him, for us and for Hitchin Town Football Club, he was posted to the relative safety of the Herts and Beds Signal Corps. There, he learned many things, relating to maths and signals and radio, but, as he often told us, he learnt most importantly that he "was as good as anyone else".

Having met my mother in South London during the war, and married her at the end of it, he brought her with him. Very soon he acquired a much higher status job, as an insurance agent for the Prudential Insurance Company. As a "Man from the Pru" he earned a secure and respectable salary, and yet, he still cycled everywhere for many years on his rounds, until we finally had our first car.

He worked hard and we rarely saw him during the week. As an insurance agent he collected the weekly premiums in cash, at the front door. To catch people in he worked his rounds at lunch time or in the evening. For us children this was just normality, but it added to my mother's feeling of isolation that he was absent so much. He rarely returned in the evening before we were put to bed.

With my older sister Sue, and my younger brother Geoff, and my mother looking after us, I felt no loneliness, but close, protected, warm, squabbling security on those long, dark winter evenings. We played and bickered and ate around the flickering coal fire in the weak electric light of that living room, the television droning on in the background, whether we were watching it or not.

Sue was my main adversary. Bookish and clever, she was thin but taller than me and I could never quite get the upper hand. She could speak sharply and sarcastically, and, as the boy, I couldn't just thump her. It always seemed unfair that she was often in the right and I was blamed when we argued. Sue was a successful student and had passed her eleven plus. As a result, she went to the Hitchin Girls' Grammar School and was the first in either Mum's or Dad's family to go to grammar school. They were very proud of her. Unlike me she liked reading and argued a lot about things in the newspaper. I found that a bit boring, as I preferred to be outside, on the move, playing and running.

But, as for Geoff, four years younger, and no good at football at all, not even very interested in sports, he was the object of my teasing. Of course, I wasn't cruel, but was just having fun and he was oversensitive anyway. He was good at drawing and made models from cardboard. I had no patience for this, nor did Dad, who never understood him. With his curly locks and freckled face, Geoff was definitely Mum's favourite, who was very protective of him. She liked me, for sure, but Geoff got all the attention. I didn't mind. I was Dad's favourite, "Frank Junior," while Geoff got little attention from Dad, who was not unkind but had little sympathy with his artistic inclinations.

Most days we gathered around the small wooden box that housed the magical television screen for children's hour. Black and white and often foggy, our temperamental entertainer was like an opiate. It gave out a stream of cartoons, such as Mickey Mouse, Popeye the Sailor Man, and cowboys – Roy Rogers and Trigger, the Lone Ranger and Tonto. Did they form our moral values? At least Popeye would overcome the dastardly Bluto and the noble cowboys would win in the end against the savage Indians, who scalped people. There was certainty that civilisation would overcome primitive savagery.

Best of all the TV offered football matches, late at night, when I would be allowed dispensation to stay up late to watch a murky picture of England playing Hungary or Poland, or Manchester United taking on some strange sounding unpronounceable team from Romania or Bulgaria. The camera was always so far away from the action and the play seemed almost to be in slow motion, the commentators so prim and proper.

Mealtimes could not interrupt the early evening ritual of Children's Hour TV. So we sat on the sofa or the deep armchair that Dad used, with our meals perched precariously on our laps. Weekday evening fare was simple and quick to prepare – boiled eggs, baked beans on toast, spaghetti on toast. This was of course tinned spaghetti, chopped up and drowning in tomato sauce. On good nights it was spaghetti with chipolatas. It was quite exotic and foreign.

Sometimes we had soup, tinned again, or just toasted cheese, made delicious with a topping of marmite or

Worcester sauce. Occasionally we enjoyed toast and dripping, left over from the previous weekend's roast, but I had to make sure I was first to get the rich gravy from the bottom of the lard bowl, for the rest was just white and tasteless.

Some evenings were special and eagerly anticipated. On Fridays Dad would always return home in the evening from work with generous portions of fish and chips he had bought on the way, carried three miles on his bike from the nearest chippie. Still steaming as they were unwrapped from the newspaper, the battered cod and greasy chips would reek of hot fat. Then came the inevitable arguing over who had the largest piece of fish or the most chips. Doused in vinegar, and eaten with bread and butter, from the paper with our fingers – what meal could be better or more warming on a bleak winter evening.

On the weekends Mum had more time to cook and meals were substantial and eaten at the table. Proper meat and two vegetable meals, freshly prepared and repetitive. Sausage and mash with peas, toad in the hole, pork or lamb chops and boiled potato and cabbage. Liver and onions and boiled potato and carrots. The best was when Mum prepared her steak and kidney pie. Succulent meat and kidney in a rich gravy, with carrot and onion, covered in a crusty pastry that no-one but my mother could create. I liked the stews too. "White" lamb stew, with chunks of greasy lamb, simmered with carrots, potato and onion, and, my favourite, ball shaped stodgy dumplings.

Wholesome, fresh, unimaginative and plentiful food; we ate well and never felt hungry. It didn't occur to me that it would ever be otherwise.

But on bad days, at my father's wh3im, there were kippers. Foul-smelling and full of scratching bones – which were so dangerous, life-threatening as you could choke on them, annoying and impossible to detect. This fish was my least favourite and had I not been so greedy I would have gone on hunger strike. Instead I had to make do with a temporary sulk.

Saturday evenings were also special. On this day the family shared a pound of toffees while watching TV together. Inevitable squabbles among my sister, my brother and me if the numbers did not share out equally or we couldn't get our favourite flavours. The programmes on TV were better on Saturdays, or seemed to be, with a choice between the BBC and ITV, though Dad said ITV was rubbish. Mum, however, liked the serials such as *Crossroads*, about a kind of hotel. I thought it was soft and didn't like romantic stuff. Everyone talked in a boring, sad voice. I favoured *I Love Lucy* and Dad preferred *Sergeant Bilko*, but I didn't get the jokes about that American army soldier. The jokes were too grown up.

Usually, we had to go to bed before TV came to an end, but if for some reason we were allowed to stay up to watch the end of a film or a football match, the programming finished about eleven o'clock, when the national anthem brought proceedings to an end, and reluctantly we dragged ourselves upstairs into the cold.

Sundays were best of all. Sundays began with a long lay-in. No-one, even my father, who was an obsessive early riser, appeared before nine o'clock. This was the most comforting day, with no school or no chores, or no programme enforced by my parents. From early on the wonderful odour of frying bacon permeated the whole house. A huge breakfast was underway. Eggs, bacon, sausage, tomato, mushrooms, fried bread, tomato ketchup and brown sauce. In the background, loud and intrusive, the radio, blaring out the popular entertainment programmes of the day. *Billy Cotton's Band Show*, with Billy Cotton roaring out his famous "Wakie Wakie!" call to announce the start. *The Navy Lark*, *Round the Horn*, which was "pretty near the mark" sometimes, according to Dad, but I never heard anything wrong with it.

Having gorged on this feast, at around eleven a.m., we could then look forward to Sunday lunch, the highlight of the week's eating, which would be set for about two p.m. As a result of this continuous eating, my mother was trapped in the kitchen for most of the day, either cooking or washing up. Dad helped sometimes, but he also had to go the pub Sunday lunch time to meet his friend Dick Hart. Mum never asked us children to help, so I never thought it necessary, though my sister lent a hand sometimes.

For lunch we always had a substantial joint of meat pork, lamb or beef. This was definitely expected of any decent family and Sunday lunch was a rite. Meat with Brussels or peas, carrots or cabbage, boiled and roast potatoes, and Yorkshire pudding, along with thick dark gravy, made from the fat of the meat and Bisto powder with Oxo cubes. Leftovers from the joint, and there usually were leftovers – were kept and cooled, ready for Monday's dinner. Minced and flavoured with onion and served with potatoes and peas, this was another delicious meal.

Sundays meant a proper dessert too. Mum made rhubarb or gooseberry tart, from garden or hedgerow ingredients, served with custard made from powder. Or if she didn't want to prepare that, we had tinned fruit with carnation cream, my favourite being peaches in syrup.

Having over-eaten for two meals the family then sank down to a soporific afternoon, as the winter darkness crept in early to paralyse all action, while the coal fire crackled and radiated uneven heat. Dad, reading the paper or snoozing in his armchair, enjoyed his main rest of the week, while Mum, finally, could sit, in her apron, and watch the Sunday afternoon film. Many of these didn't interest me, about love and romance, or musicals, which I thought too superficial. But when the cowboy or the war films came on, I was transfixed. *High Noon* and *The Cockleshell Heroes* provided me with my boyhood role models. I was conscious of wondering if I would be brave like James Stewart or the British Commandoes if I was faced with such overwhelming odds. I thought I would and my games of imagination confirmed my confidence. I would be brave when I joined the army.

After the nadir of my week, Saturday night and Sunday afternoon, came the anti-climax of a Sunday evening, as dreary, depressing and full of foreboding as the thought of another week of school loomed like a spectre in my mind. Not that school itself was so awful, but how much more preferable to avoid the challenge and demands of school and stay within the passive cotton wool protection of our family living room.

Even TV programming was designed to invoke melancholia. How I disliked *Songs of Praise* with its dreary organ music and mournful hymn singing, like an antidote to joy. Dad said he didn't believe in it all, though Jesus was probably a good man who inspired people. Mum liked the singing though, so the TV stayed on. The last hope of entertainment lay with *Sunday Night at the London Palladium*, but I mostly pretended to watch this so it delayed the inevitable call to bath time and bedtime and the end of all sluggish happiness for another week.

Bath time was uncomfortable and a duty to be endured as quickly as possible. There was never enough hot water, as the only heating came from the coal fire downstairs. Such water as we had was only lukewarm, and, anyway, in the family pecking order I had to wait until my sister Sue had finished her bath. I particularly hated having my hair washed as the shampoo always stung my eyes. A miserable single bar electric heater provided the only source of comfort in an otherwise bare and chilly bathroom. Getting out of the increasingly cold water was a torture. The only answer was to hurriedly put on vest, pyjamas, dressing gown and slippers as close to the electric fire as possible without setting alight to any clothing and rush to the bedroom, where Mum had already put a hot water bottle into the bed. Mercifully, bath time was only once a week, on Sunday nights. The rest of the week only face and hands were washed regularly, though I had the kitchen sink ritual sometimes to bear. No-one thought a weekly bath unusual. All my friends did the same and none of them seemed to smell too badly, apart from the Potter boys, but they were common anyway.

Our clothes would be made ready for the week. Vests were always worn, underneath school white shirt and school pullover, grey with blue and yellow piping, and a school tie, blue with horizontal yellow stripes. Grey shorts, all year round, and long grey socks. This was the uniform, which remained unchanged, literally, for a week's schooling. Clothes were neatly laid out at the bottom of the bed so we could dress quickly in the morning.

I never liked going to bed. It seemed to be cold most of the time, very dark and deeply silent. The village peace was broken some nights only by the howling or whistling wind, which was eerie. Sometimes an owl would hoot from the park land opposite, and it seemed so mournful and creepy, I would pull the thick blankets and eiderdown over my head, so that I was well protected against any intruding murderers or monsters. I wasn't scared of course, and Mum and Dad were downstairs to protect us. On those nights, however, when they had gone to bed before I slept, there was an added insecurity. Obviously, anyone could break into the front door and rush up the stairs and turn left into our bedroom before Dad could get up to stop them. Sometimes, I crept out onto the landing, pretending to go the toilet, and just hung about outside their bedroom door, which they always left open, hoping they would hear the creaking floorboards under my feet, and offer to let me sleep with them, as I did when I was smaller. But if they awoke, Dad would scold me. "Go back to bed, you'll catch your death of cold", he would say. "You're not a baby any more". Humiliated, I would excuse myself with the toilet justification, and then slope miserably back to bed.

The scary dreams often involved gorillas. Had I seen them on some TV nature programme? Why were they after me? Perhaps King Kong was on the loose again. And those strange visions of Auntie Doreen chasing me, her jaw jutting out in ugly, threatening fashion. Her cancerous jaw, pointing like a weapon as she chased me. Was she trying to stab me? Philip Cooper would chase me in my dreams and very nearly catch me. There were the good dreams too, when Luton Town were short of a player and asked me, from the crowd, to stand in for them. Alongside my hero Billy Bingham I would play and Billy would put me through with an inch perfect pass and the goalkeeper was rushing out, the crowd cheering........ it was one to one!

Then, too soon, my consciousness was gently prised open by the plink, plink, plink of "Oh what a beautiful morning" and I had to stretch out into the cold air to turn off the alarm and bring the petite, twirling ballerina to a stop. There was ice on the inside of the window and another day had begun.

Chapter Two
What's in a Name?

A distinguished theologian of the third century, he was renowned for his learning and eloquence. He gained both fame and notoriety, before suffering a grisly end. Having probably been a prison warder at some early stage of his career, he was self-taught, and became sufficiently immodest in his beliefs to declare himself Bishop of Rome in opposition to the sitting Pope of his day. In this way Hippolytus of Rome gained the dubious distinction of being the very first anti-Pope.

Born in 170 AD, Hippolytus was converted to Christianity as a young man and soon threw himself energetically into the doctrinal and liturgical disputes that characterised the early years of this new religion. Greek speaking and writing in that language, he authored many tracts and several books dealing with such thorny theoretical issues as the nature of the holy trinity, which preoccupied the scholars of the budding church. Unfortunately, only fragments of his works survive, though we do have accounts from chroniclers of the fourth century making reference to his views.

He was particularly exercised by the dispute that surrounded the treatment of new converts. Some in the infant church's hierarchy, including the Popes Urban and

Pontian, favoured relaxing the penitential system for those newly enlightened pagans. This made it easier to forgive them when they lapsed into slyly worshipping, or retaining, their heathen idols and practices. It probably seemed like a sensible recruiting policy.

Hippolytus and his likeminded followers, however, would have none of it and disputed publicly with the Pope. This schism led to his unilateral declaration of Popish independence from Pontian and his being labelled a heretic.

Matters then went from bad to worse. A new Roman emperor, Maximinus, took a dislike to this meddling, puritanical sect and acted ruthlessly. Both Pontian and Hippolytus were exiled to the mines of Sardinia in 235 AD. Hippolytus was sentenced to death. But no ordinary death. According to later reports stemming from the fourth century he was condemned to be torn apart, limb from limb, by horses.

Whether true or not, this bloody equine dismemberment gained Hippolytus not only reconciliation with the Church but martyrdom status and sainthood. The corpse was retrieved and returned to Rome. He became the patron saint of prisons, prison warders and horses, on account of his chequered history and sacrificial fate, and to this day his Saint Day is August 13th.

The nature of his martyrdom, as it was reported several centuries later, reflected the origins of his name. Hippolytus is Greek, meaning "Driver or Unleasher of Horses", "Hippo" being "horse", as in "Hippopotamus", meaning river horse.

In Greek mythology the most famous Hippolytus of all did not have a happy lot. Born illegitimately from the rape of Hippolyta, the queen of the Amazons, by Theseus, the

King of Athens, he nevertheless looked set for a comfortable life as a member of the aristocracy.

However, as so often happened in Greek legends, the gods intervened with malevolent intent, and Hippolytus's fate was sealed. It all began to go wrong when Theseus married Phaedra (yes, Racine's famous Phedre). Hippolytus' new stepmother took an unhealthy fancy to her adopted son, egged on by the mischievous goddess Aphrodite, whom Hippolytus had rejected.

Our noble youth, however, being chaste and honourable, angrily repulsed his new mother's amorous advances out of hand. This, and the guilt she suffered, destroyed her. She refused to eat and died of a broken heart and shame. However, a note was found on her body which wreaked revenge on Hippolytus, claiming the youth had raped here.

Mad with disgust, Theseus exiled his son, but also orchestrated his death. Being part of a Greek myth this naturally took a highly imaginative and spectacular form. Simply putting him to death would not have been dramatic enough.

Instead, Theseus turned to Poseidon, the God of the Ocean, who happened to be his father and owed him three wishes. Poseidon was requested to bring about the end of the innocent young man. To carry out this unfortunate and totally unrighteous act, Poseidon summoned up a frightening sea monster in the shape of a bull.

At Poseidon's command, this terrifying creature burst from the ocean, just as Hippolytus was making his sad way into exile along the seashore in his chariot. His steeds were driven crazy by the sudden appearance of this monstrosity and bolted. The chariot overturned, and poor Hippolytus was caught in the traces and dragged onto the rocks, where his body was battered and broken. Too late, Theseus found out the truth. His dying son was brought to him, forgave him but then expired.

We know about this edifying tale from the Greek playwright Euripides, whose play Hippolytus brought together the strands of various legends into a harrowing drama for the entertainment of the Athenians in the fourth century BC.

Some six hundred years later, our theologian and anti-pope bearing the same name was to endure a similar fate to Euripides' protagonist. We have to speculate whether this was the result of some perverse decision of Emperor Maximinus, or the fertile creativity of Christian commentators many years later. Perhaps they wished to feed the myth of the martyr with an execution reflecting the legends surrounding his name.

Whatever the facts, Hippolytus was to gain lasting sainthood. Like other saints he would be remembered through prayers and a saint day. Chapels and churches would be dedicated to him throughout Christendom – including an 11th century church on an obscure hilltop lying among the rolling Chiltern Hills of North Hertfordshire in far off Britain.

Chapter Three
World Outside

We spent the majority of our time outdoors. Winter and summer, most children of the village, as long as they were not ill or weak, played outside in their free time. There were no fears of paedophiles or weirdos or even traffic, which was only a problem if you went near the main London road to Hitchin. Otherwise, the entire village, with its lanes and alleys, greens and allotments, fields and hedgerows, was our vast playground, across which we ranged with freedom and unchecked imagination. The only limitation came when the mothers' calls came through the warm summer air or the misty evening of autumn or the chill of a winter afternoon: "Come and get your tea! Tea's ready!

First gathering place for us, and scene of early socialisation outside the family, was the recreation ground, or "The rec" as everyone called it. Fortunately for us, and all the families who lived in Waterdell Lane, our rear gardens backed onto this green adventure area, which I could access through a hole in the hedge. At the top of the rec was a children's play area, with two sets of swings, one for the young ones – from which I had long graduated – and a tall set of six. We also had a see-saw – a kind of swinging log – from which we would hurl ourselves onto the grass nearby, and a roundabout, which we aimed to spin at the highest speed possible in order to make the youngsters cry out with alarm or get so dizzy they fell over.

Here I formed my first friendships and experienced my earliest enmities and disputes. The children were like me, from village families, some of many generations. White, solid Anglo-Saxon, rural stock. So David Jenkins, Graham Russell, Tony, Martin, Colin, Eric, Peter and others formed an amorphous gang. Whoever was around and available could be part of the game or match that was improvised.

There were girls too. Generally tomboyish and tough, the village girls could hold their own. They were good at cartwheels and climbing to the top of the frame of the big swings, from which they would hang upside down with their legs hooked over the top bar. Usually wearing print dresses, with cardigans and white socks and sandals, they would tuck their dresses into their underwear so that we couldn't see their knickers when they were upside down and tease them. But as they didn't play football or war games, they remained mostly separate from the boys, which was normal.

This was almost always a harmonious scene. There were few serious fights or arguments. There was space enough for all. But just occasionally it was spoilt, usually by Tony McGowan. He was the bully we all disliked, but he enjoyed his status. Tony was about fourteen, older than most of us, who were around ten or eleven. He would interrupt our games and insist on joining in, though as he was stronger and taller, he would dominate, whether it was football or tag or paddle. If we protested, he would use Chinese burns on our wrists till we cried, or Irish whips, twisting our arms up our backs till we agreed to his wishes. We would try to keep away from him, but he would follow us, even when we hid at the bottom of the rec.

Once, when he had made me cry, I told Dad, and he went round to the McGowans' house to complain. But when he came back he was red-faced and angry and said that the McGowans were rude people and that he had had an argument with them. The McGowans lived next door to my friend David Jenkins, and Anne Jenkins, his mother, said that Tony wasn't all bad and that we should let him play with us. We just thought that the adults had no understanding of the situation and that they wouldn't do anything about Tony.

Regardless of these occasional setbacks, our village playground community enjoyed great freedom from fear and from parental control. We explored the entire parish, over fields and allotments, back lanes and woods, spinneys and streams and ponds, in our imaginative games and adventures. Our activities were heavily influenced by the two main themes war and sport.

World War Two had only been over about fifteen years. Our parents' generation had been actively involved in it as soldiers or civilians. Even our quiet village had been directly affected, with eight young men killed. All fit men, like my father, had been conscripted and served for six long years. Civilians, like my mother, who grew up in South London, lived their prime years of youth through bombing raids, doodlebugs, blackouts, rationing, fear and uncertainty.

We fifties' generation grew up basking in the aftermath of victory. There was no qualification or revisions to the total moral superiority of the Allies. The brave Tommy, aided by the Americans, and temporarily the Russians (though they were certainly under suspicion) had defeated the evil Germans and Japanese. We were constantly fed this version of history through films, TV, radio and comics.

Churchillian rhetoric inspired us. Our heroes were the "the Few" of the Battle of Britain, the Desert Rats, the Dunkirk little ships, the D-Day troops, the Paratroopers of Arnhem, glorious in defeat, and the Chindits of Burma, who were led by none other than Orde Wingate. Like David Niven, they were suave, unruffled, ice-cool and spoke in clipped upper class accents.

The enemy, on the other hand, were bestial and certainly not gentlemen. German soldiers had a limited vocabulary. "Englische Schweinhund" and "Hande hoch" were part of it, along with the more frequent "Kamaraden", meaning surrender. Even more despised, the Japanese were hated because of the ill-treatment they had meted out to British prisoners of war. The animosity was slightly tempered by the pity engendered following scenes of the suffering after the Hiroshima A-bombs. Nevertheless, "Japs" could only shout "Banzai" and indulge in suicide attacks.

Not surprisingly, everyone preferred to be the British army in our war games, rather than the "Huns" or the "Nips". As many as twenty or thirty might take part in one of these exercises at times. Occasionally some girls took part too.

Having divided in two armies, everyone had to be armed. The most sophisticated had plastic replica Tommy guns or rifles, but they were the few. I had a Tommy gun for a while, but it depended on batteries to keep the red tube, representing fire from the barrel, vibrating. Once the batteries ran out, it was a bit embarrassing. For the majority, the weaponry was simpler – a piece of wood, say eighteen inches long, with a short piece nailed on at right angles as the magazine, and a length of string as the shoulder strap. Really lucky or spoilt friends even had plastic army helmets or replica combat jackets.

Suitably armed, the battle would begin. It would last hours and stretch over many miles. We could drive the enemy two miles down Maydencroft Lane at the edge of our village, to the hamlet of Charlton, or retreat three across the allotments to Preston woods, or skirmish among the trees of the Park up to Almshoe Bury. The aim was to drive the enemy back. If you succeeded in shooting someone, you would shout "Got you" – and it was accepted, the victim would roll in dramatic death throes on the ground, probably taking several pirouettes beforehand, until collapsing with loud groans. He would then have to count up to at least twenty, slowly, before being able to take part again. Consequently, the war games never reached definitive endings.

It was allowed to hurl clods of earth, or sods of grass, as hand grenades at the enemy, but stones were definitely forbidden. We dug trenches and foxholes, we charged across cow fields, yelling blood-curdling war cries, and we mimicked the sounds of rifle fire, machine guns and exploding grenades.

In Graham Russell's backyard we built an earth fort. Luckily, his father didn't care for gardening anyway, so we dug a three-foot-deep trench at the end of the garden and piled up the debris to form a rampart in front of it. This we topped with sods of grass. Behind this fortification, we brave British Tommies held out against waves of bloodthirsty Japanese attacks, hurling clumps of wet earth as grenades against our enemies. Many a valiant hour was passed in this way. Only when I was bitten by Graham's spaniel did this particular fantasy adventure come to an end as I refused to go around there again.

Less bloodthirsty, but equally competitive, were the sports-based games. Sport dominated the annual calendar. It seemed that everyone was engaged, whether it be soccer, cricket, horseracing, tennis, motor racing, golf or boxing. All had their moments in the year and we crowded around the TV or radio as our heroes and heroines showed the world how it was done. It was the FA Cup, or the Test Match, or Wimbledon, or the Grand National that saw us through the routine of the year.

The British loved sport. Perhaps it was a reaction against the drab, fearful days of the war. Or perhaps the establishment really did avoid revolution by participating in it with the hoi-poloi. Non-political sport, with glamour and celebrities, was a relief and escape from the realities of Cold War and nuclear threat. Not only that, Britain was clearly superior in most sports. After all, Roger Bannister had run the first four-minute mile. Stirling Moss was World Champion, wasn't he? True, Hungary's football maestros had thrashed us at Wembley, and the USA had knocked us out of the World Cup, but even at soccer we played the game in the bravest, most honest way.

We played football endlessly. At all opportunities. On all occasions. At all venues. It might be a proper football that someone had got for Christmas, kicked around on the rec. But it could easily be a tennis ball, bouncing around the school yard. It didn't matter how many took part. Three could play, with one in goal and one against one. Lose the ball and the tackler retreats twenty yards and you start again. Come rain or shine, mud or dust, football was an obsession.

Inspired by the British sporting calendar, our games also included cricket and running. If a major test match against Australia or the West Indies was attracting national interest, then we were suddenly aspiring Colin Cowdreys or Ted Dexters, the heroes of the day. Cricket never captured my imagination as much as football, however, because I wasn't so good at it.

I would play one to ones with Colin Stubbs at the bottom of the rec, as Colin had a full cricket set, including proper stumps, bails and even pads. The problem was, I would seem to be bowling endlessly, while he whacked the ball a hundred yards away. That meant I had to trot after it, retrieve it and then pad back to bowl again. If ever I managed to get him out, my stay at the crease would inevitably be short lived, because he was a much better bowler than me. When there were more of us playing, I nevertheless seemed to spend hours daydreaming in the field, only to miss the rare catching chance when it came my way.

We did on one occasion organise our own Olympics, shortly after the Rome Olympics. We crudely marked out a hundred-yard track in the rec with sticks stuck into the ground and decided that a complete lap around the field was equivalent to 880 yards. The only problem was that a couple of the boys kept winning everything. Martin Saich was the better sprinter, so the rest of us gave up after a couple of races. Then Graham Russell easily won the longer races. After a while, us also-rans developed a sulk and refused to take part any further. We hadn't quite imbued the true Olympic spirit.

At certain times of the year, there were other diversions, not necessarily so legal. Scrumping was acceptable, and not really considered a form of theft. Stealing apples from the orchard at the bottom of the rec seemed fair game. We were quite conscious of the fact that it was wrong, and that we would be scolded, if not punished, when caught. But we considered it a normal pastime of a village boy. Hadn't every generation done it? What's more, I don't remember ever being caught red-handed at the orchard. We had a well-developed system. Three or four of us would perch ourselves in a tree on the rec side of the hedge separating it from the orchard. From here we had a wide view of the approaches all around and could see anyone coming from quite far, particularly from the orchard side, from where the farmer could appear. Having made sure that the coast was clear, two or three would scamper down the tree, through a gap in the hedge and launch an attack on the nearest apple tree. Low boughs would be shaken, and sticks hurled at the higher branches. When enough fruit had fallen or been picked, pockets and jumpers loaded, the miscreants would scramble back through the hedge and clamber up the original tree. The whole slick operation would take about three minutes, exhilarating on account of its brazen criminality. A feast on the hoard of the twenty or so apples that had been secured would follow. Almost invariably, that would be followed an hour or two later by acute stomach ache, and guilt feelings as we lied to our mothers as to the cause of our pain.

Less acceptable was scrumping in the allotments. There were several allotment patches in the village, one being immediately behind David Jenkins' back garden, which made it a soft target as we could dash in and out of the family's yard. Our objective would be garden peas, or sometimes strawberries, or even carrots. On one occasion we were found out – caught in the act by Mr Youngman, who had a particularly fine crop of peas. He was lying in wait and chased us away. We were too quick to be caught, but he knew exactly who we were.

Sure enough, that evening, he was knocking at our door and complaining to my father about our raids on his allotment. As Dad didn't especially like Mr Youngman, and although he listened politely to him and agreed that our behaviour was unacceptable and would have to stop, he administered a mild ticking off. I was made to understand that raiding allotments, on which people worked hard to grow extra food, was not scrumping but stealing. I never did it again. We carried on our raids for apples, however, for that didn't carry the same ethical negativity... and we never got caught.

I was on the end of a much more serious scolding, however, because of Philip Cooper. Philip, who was a Down's Syndrome boy, or as everyone called it then, a Mongol, was about eighteen years old. He often sat on the small children's swings, humming to himself and fiddling with his handkerchief. He looked strange to us, with unusual eyes, big nose and lips. In temperament he was quite harmless and gentle, and the kinder boys and girls would sit with him and he would hug them. To some of us though, he was an object of suspicion. I was frightened of him, because he was unpredictable and, also, strong. There were rumours that if he caught you when he was mad, he would strangle you. Sometimes we would call him names... "Coopy Loopy", "Loopy Coopy" and so on. He would sometimes react and chase us away, but he couldn't move very fast and we would always escape.

On one occasion, along with a couple of other boys, I began teasing him. From the safety of a row of garages, which lay behind the swings where he sat, we called out to him and threw small stones to irritate him. The aim was to get him to chase us and enjoy the thrill of a dangerous chase. With the row of garages to dash in and out of, we felt quite sure we could elude him. At first he shouted to us to stop, and then, when we continued, he got up, turned round and started towards us. We three scrambled away, all in different directions. I ran back along the narrow gap between two garages, then swerved back down the alleyway between the next two, sure that my manoeuvre would ensure my escape. However, I was brought to a sudden halt, seeing that my passageway had been sealed off at the end with a makeshift barbed wire fence. Alarmed, I turned to retrace my steps, only to see my pursuer coming into the passageway. I was trapped! This could be the end of me!

In panic I turned again and pulled at the barbed wire to make a hole large enough to wriggle through. In the effort I cut my hands, and then, as I pushed through the fence head first, scratched my forehead and tore my sweater. No matter, this was life or death. Finally, cutting my legs and grazing my knees, I scrambled free and ran like a demon for home.

In my dishevelled and distraught state I confessed to teasing Philip and being chased by him. My mother, knowing the background to this, guessed who was in the wrong. Once I had recovered from my trauma I was shocked again on being told I had to go with my mother to the Coopers to apologise to Philip. Shamefaced, I was marched over to their council house on the other side of the rec. I mumbled an apology as directed by my mother. Mrs Cooper was understanding, while Philip, to my horror, gave me a hug. The experience caused me to think, and I never indulged in tormenting him again, though I remained cautious and kept my distance in case he strangled me in revenge.

As in this case, I generally accepted my parents' moral code without question, but one incident, when I was about eleven, did test my loyalty. After yet another squabble with my older sister, Sue, I overreacted and whacked her across the top of her eye with my fist. This was the only time I ever hit her, and I can't remember why my feelings were so strong. She ran crying to my mother while I made myself scarce. Parental response was unusually strict, however, as Sue's eye reddened then turned into a colourful "shiner". Mum told me off, but worse followed when Dad returned home and he angrily rebuked me and sent me to my room. I had never really experienced this level of discipline and to me it appeared very unjust. After all, hadn't my sister provoked me? Wasn't she older, anyway? And why be so abnormally harsh with me?

My sense of injustice motivated me to hatch a plot that would teach them all a lesson. I would run away. That would demonstrate just how hurt I was by the victimisation I was suffering. It needed careful planning. I aimed to depart in the early evening. It was summer, so the day was long. I would then hide in the "camp" we had in the thick bushes at the bottom of the rec. This wasn't too far away and I thought I would be well-hidden from the inevitable anxious search for me, once I failed to return home for tea. I would disappear for a whole night, so one major problem was my fear of the dark. To overcome my anxiety I hit on the idea of inviting a friend to join me. Francis Porter, a classmate and friend in my class at school, agreed to join me and our Huckleberry Finn adventure began to take shape.

I gradually collected, secretly of course, the materials for the expedition, in the bottom drawer of my bedroom chest. Extra socks, old sweater and felt cowboy hat for warmth. A Mars bar, an orange and peanuts for provisions. To make my point for justice and fairness I also wrote a note to my parents, to be found after my disappearance. Yes, this would make it clear that they would lose me – this time for one night only, because I aimed to return the next day – if they maltreated me again. I pointed out that they always favoured my sister, because she was a girl and that they had been unfair to me.

As the agreed day for the breakout approached I became quite nervous. The idea of spending all night in the camp was unsettling, but necessary. On the day itself I hastened to go round to Francis Porter's in the late afternoon to confirm final arrangements for that evening. But it resulted in disappointment, for Francis had completely forgotten about the plan. Anyway, he explained, he was having his tea and it was his favourite – baked beans on toast. I returned home, heroically dispirited but inwardly relieved. There was no way I was going to spend the night in that hole in the ground on my own! Francis had provided a reasonable excuse to abandon the project.

However, I was mistaken thinking the affair was over, for when I arrived home, my father sat me down for a serious talking to. They had found the evidence of my planned adventure, including the note, and my mother was very upset. He wasn't angry, so much as sad that I had caused my mother any distress. He asked me if I had really intended to run away. "Not really," I explained. Dad pointed out that I had been in the wrong, hitting my sister like that, and that I should go and explain things to my mother. I had a distinct feeling that he didn't take my plot very seriously. In fact, I think he was quite amused.

Not so my mother, who was genuinely tearful that her son felt his upbringing was so unbearable that he even contemplated deserting the comfort of home. However, I was genuinely remorseful that I had caused her this grief and with half the truth pointed out that I had no intention of actually carrying it through. Soon all was peace again, to my relief. I never concocted such a plan again, nor did I punch my sister!

At least the camp at the bottom of the recreation ground, hidden away in the bushes, remained in regular use and its secret nature meant it proved a useful location for my first experiment in sexual discovery. David Jenkins and I arranged with Jeanie Porter and Madie Bryden that we should meet there to show each other our private parts. This was deliciously naughty and forbidden. The inspection, however, was something of an anti-climax. There didn't appear to be anything particularly interesting in a girl's fanny, as we called it. In fact, there wasn't really anything there. I did realise the connection with making babies, though it remained something of a mystery. I understood that poking a girl with your finger was a fuck and that poking her with your willy was a shag, though it all seemed quite pointless.

Tony McGowan, who was older than us, had talked about sexual intercourse, but this was evidently ridiculous and quite disgusting. My mother and father would never have indulged in that kind of behaviour, and, anyway, could you possibly imagine the Queen and Prince Philip dong it? Anne Jenkins, David's mum, had provided the most sensible and re-assuring explanation of the mysteries of life. Men and women, she had explained to David, when they were married and in love, would cuddle and kiss at night in bed. During this process the man's balls would transfer into the woman's body and then grow into babies. This was an acceptable and affectionate solution to the problem, though if we had thought it through we might have wondered how the transfer took place and why some families had more than two children.

At times, we ventured beyond the security of the rec to explore the outer reaches of our parish. Beyond the village of Gosmore lay the dark pond, which had a dangerous atmosphere. Although only some 30 feet across, it lay in woods in permanent gloom. It probably wasn't that deep, but that didn't stop us imagining deadly monsters skulking in the murky waters. It was also surrounded by black, glutinous mud. No doubt it would suck you under like quicksand and devour you without trace. All this made the pond an attractive and exciting place. At one time a group of us decided to conquer this menace by building a causeway across the mud and water. We patiently collected straw, grasses, twigs and branches and piled them to form a pathway across. The effort lasted a week or more of regular visits, but each time we returned the evil pond had absorbed the previous day's efforts. I don't think we ever managed to stretch the causeway more than about three yards. The evil spell of the place was thus unbroken.

Another enchanted place with an aura of peril was the old ice house. This was an ancient underground brick built structure near St Ibbs Park. It receded far underground, though we never dared venture too far inside as it was unlit and menacing, blocked by rubble and refuse. Rumours and myths surrounded this place. Some said that Italian prisoners of war had tunnelled out from the adjacent field, which had been a camp, to make their escape. Others claimed it led underground to the nearby manor house, providing a means of escape for the local gentry in times of political upheaval. More unlikely, another tale had it leading for a mile under the park, up the hill, to the church! The stories made it enticing. For us, it served as a Neanderthal cave dwelling, in which we sat having secret feasts, hidden from the prying eyes of adults – or so we thought.

Secret parties involved fires and food. There was an old oil drum, in which we placed straw and twigs as fuel for the fire, on which we would bake potatoes, picked from the nearby allotments. This feast would be accompanied by chocolate bars and the luxury drink of the day – Tizer – purchased with specially saved up pocket money.

Secrecy, being away from adults, was a theme of many of our games, probably fuelled by Enid Blyton stories, or the adventures of Huckleberry Finn. We looked for the ultimate secret camp. Once, with a friend called Keith Bryden, I found what I thought was the ultimate hideaway. It was on the far side of the village allotments, a long way from the road and regularly used pathways. Buried deep in a thick hedge, the camp was difficult to access. You had to climb up a tree, slide along a branch, drop to the ground, then crawl through a tunnel to reach the tiny clearing, which we had chopped out of the vegetation. Like all quality secret camps, it had to be provisioned and we supplied it with an old blanket, bottles of water and comics. Sadly, our cover was blown within a couple of days. As Keith and I sat, whispering conspiratorially in our camp, a couple of girls from our class in school came meandering along the hedge line. This was the test! We would observe them, perfectly camouflaged, while they passed by, completely oblivious to our presence. It was a major disappointment when they stopped immediately opposite and greeted us with a nonchalant "Hi there, got a new camp? Can we come in?"

Other favourite locations were further afield, needing a bike ride to reach. One of these was the old mill at the end of Maydencroft Lane, on the village boundary. Here the stream ran down to the neighbouring and ancient village of Charlton. For us the mill stream was a playground, but also, in the spring, it's where we headed for tadpoling. This involved collecting jelly-like frog spawn in jam jars and transporting it home to "breed" in buckets in the back garden. Sadly, this rarely succeeded and few frogs actually emerged from the incarceration.

We also roamed the fields and woodland to the west, towards the neighbouring village of Preston. Wain wood was a well-known spot, as were the Preston "hills". Here on some sunny summer afternoons at the weekend we would proceed on foot as a family for a picnic. Encamped on the hillside, on an old blanket, we would enjoy my mother's home made picnic fare, while fighting off the wasps and flies. Egg and cucumber, ham and tomato sandwiches; pork pie, jam tarts, boiled eggs, lemonade, tea from a thermos flask. We would all play French cricket, until I squabbled too much with my sister and brother, or one of us would sulk at being out. Dad would then lie down to snooze on the grass while Mum flicked through a magazine. Us children would try to catch butterflies or make daisy chains. Lazy, innocent afternoons untroubled by time or responsibility, were interrupted only by the drone of wandering bumble bees.

Another type of family expedition, which my sister and I found exciting, was going mushrooming, because this involved getting up at the crack of dawn and trekking out to the cow pastures around the village. In late summer or early autumn we would be out early, especially after a rainy night, in our Wellington boots, with my father, scouring the grass for field mushrooms. It had to be early, or they would shrivel in the hot sun of the day. And it had to be wet and humid, for that was when they best sprouted overnight. We had to be careful to pick the right ones, for some were poisonous. They had to be white on top and black underneath the hood. Certainly not brown – they were toadstools and would make you sick. We would collect a whole plastic shopping bag full and take them home triumphantly. Mum would then fry a great pile of them, which would be greedily devoured with bacon, fried eggs and bread and butter.

Generally, we confined ourselves to the boundaries of the village. Once, when I ventured further afield, with my sister, on our bikes, we experienced an unpleasant outcome. We rode the three miles to nearby Preston village, where we rested a while on the picturesque village green, before heading back down the lane that led home. But just outside the village we were held up by a group of Preston boys, perhaps thirteen or fourteen years old. They blocked the road with a long log and threatened us. They demanded money and we had to give them the few pence we had. Still they wouldn't let us pass. In the end we had no choice but to turn around to go through the centre of the village and exit by another lane, which also headed to St Ippolyts, but was several miles longer.

When we finally got home, exhausted and distressed, we told of our ordeal and my father was upset to hear the story. He made us get into the car immediately and off we went in search of the young bullies. We drove to Preston and circled around looking for the culprits. It was, however, all in vain. They had disappeared and as the evening drew in we returned home. I was quite glad we didn't find the boys, as I didn't like confrontation and I was worried it might cause problems in the future, if we came across them again.

The lesson was learned. Better to stay within the safe domain of our own St. Ippolyts, where people knew us and where life was orderly and civilised.

Chapter Four
Settlers

By the eighth century the undulating country that three hundred years later formed the parish of St Ippolyts was under the control of a local tribe called the Hicce or Hwicce (probably pronounced "Hitchy"). They gave their name to the nearby market town, long since known as Hitchin. Fields that would belong to the village were at that time best patchily farmed or used as grazing pasture, and almost certainly still heavily wooded.

We know about the Hicce from an ancient document, labelled the "Tribal Hidage" by historians. Originating as early as the eighth or even the seventh century, this fascinating document lists the main tribes of England which existed at that time south of the Humber. It tells us where they lived, and how powerful they were, by virtue of the "hides" of land they controlled. An indistinct measurement of land, a hide was said to be enough to sustain a free man and his family, and variously reckoned at between 40 to 120 acres.

Scholars still argue the case, but the Tribal Hidage was most likely produced for the rulers of Mercia – which kingdom, centred on the Midlands, dominated a patchwork of royal fiefdoms and lesser tribal areas in those times. It may have been a kind of record to assess the tribute these peoples would owe to Mercia – a precursor of the Domesday Book, William of Normandy's nationwide property register.

Owning just 300 hides, compared to Mercia's 30,000 or the West Saxons' 100,000, the Hicce were comparative small fry. Their name may be ancient British rather than Anglo-Saxon, but they were surely within the Mercian sphere of influence. Perhaps they had arrived with Saxon tribes who settled central England and created Mercia after the Roman withdrawal, and, moving westward inland, found the area amenable. They possibly took their name from the gently flowing river they found there – the river Hiz (originally pronounced "Hitch"), which was also British in derivation. Or, some think, they took their tribal name from a leader, Hicca.

However, by whatever route the Hicce arrived to settle this area, they were certainly not the first to tramp over these North Hertfordshire hills. In fact, the oldest known road in Britain, the Icknield Way, brushed immediately by Hitchin to the North. This prehistoric by-way linked Norfolk via a south-west route to Hampshire. Following the chalk escarpment of the Chiltern Hills it was a well-trodden trading route and pastoral highway, along which ancient farmers moved their herds and flocks. It could well have been the route by which the Hicce arrived.

Just to the East of Hitchin, a mile from the future boundary of St Ippolyts, ran the Roman Ermine Street, which connected London with York, providing one of the great arteries of the Roman province of Britain and strategic thoroughfare for its all-conquering armies. Even this road, which was to become the first numbered highway of motorised Britain, the A1, was laid over tracks trodden down in the mists of time long before the Romans. So we can be confident that his region was well explored even before they arrived.

Before Caesar's invasions in 55 and 54 BC this part of the country was the stamping ground of the Belgic Celtic tribe – the Catuvellauni. They didn't take kindly to the Roman imposition of the British king Verulamium, who was based at modern day St Albans. Under their legendary king Caractacus they rebelled, but were crushed by the legions in AD 43. They rose again to join Boadicea's Iceni uprising, only to suffer another catastrophic defeat at the hands of Roman general Suetonius. This disaster occurred at a battleground somewhere within a few miles of what was later Hitchin.

Leaving us only a few vestiges of their presence, the Romans did not colonise North Hertfordshire so much as the south, around modern-day St Albans, where the thriving town of Verulamium sprang up. However, there were scattered outposts, evidence of which can be seen in the remains of a fine villa, homestead and graveyard in the Hitchin area.

It seems that as the Romans withdrew from Britain in the 4th and 5th centuries, the Hicce were establishing themselves in this location. But the real consolidation of Hitchin as a settlement of any significance came when the greatest Mercian King, Offa – he who built the dyke to keep the marauding Welsh out – chose the site as his battle headquarters.

In 758 Offa defeated the usurper to his throne, one Beornred, in three bloody encounters in the vicinity of Hitchin. To celebrate the victory Offa built a palace in the settlement, giving it royal recognition. Offa himself did not stay long, moving to a nearby camp, a few miles distant, which evolved into the village of Offley.

However, the Mercian grandee never forgot Hitchin or the part it had played in his good fortune. As he reached the end of his life, in 792, he sought, like many a noble lord, to ensure his eternal salvation through penance, and founded a Benedictine House in the town. The monks, through prayer and solicitation, would ensure Offa a restful afterlife. Before his death he bequeathed it to a kinsman, Eadric. He, unfortunately, showed little interest in Hitchin, preferring the wealthier abode of St Albans, where he was appointed Abbott. Nevertheless, this monastery was commonly regarded as the foundation of the church, which over the next centuries developed into Hitchin's impressive St Mary's, the largest and most magnificent parish church in all of Hertfordshire.

Hitchin's fortunes over the next centuries waxed and waned. By the eighth and ninth centuries the old English kingdoms were being sorely pressed by the Viking invasions and much of Mercia was overrun. Hitchin and its surroundings lay on the disputed borderland between the Norsemen and the Saxon kingdoms of the Southwest.

Alfred the Great, after famously burning the cakes, fought back against the incursions and secured his kingdom of Wessex through the Treaty of Wedmore in 878 with the Danish king Guthrum. For Hitchin, this didn't bode well, as the town fell on the wrong side of the treaty line and was delivered into the newly established Danelaw. Sixty years later, however, it was back in Saxon hands again.

The town survived these mixed fortunes, as did its largely neglected monastery. In 910 the institution was ravaged by fire, but rebuilt again. It was widely accepted for many years that Offa's founding of the Benedictine House had laid the first foundations of Hitchin's St Mary's Church. More recent excavations showed, however, that some kind of religious building already existed on that site. Having maintained a presence then, for nearly five hundred years, the monastic site continued to operate beyond William the Conqueror's successful subjugation of Anglo-Saxon Britain in 1066.

We read of it in the Domesday Book, William's detailed survey of his newly acquired subjects and their possessions, produced in 1086. Hitchin's "monasterium" or monastery is mentioned. We also see that it held religious sway over the local parishes surrounding the town.

One of these was the parish of St Hippolytus, where, just in this same year, a new church dedicated to that saint was being raised. It was to be the focal point and foundation of a new village settlement.

Chapter Five
Arrivals

I made my trouble-free appearance on January 18, 1950, thanks to a smooth birth and the good work of the North Herts Hospital maternity unit. I was my parents' second child, my sister Sue having been born two years earlier. In the year of my arrival the Korean War was raging and rationing still operated in post-war Britain. Despite lingering austerity, it was a time of growing optimism for people like my parents. The welfare state had been established and the wretchedness of the 1930s depression and crisis of war had been survived. They had their own home, provided by the council, and my father had a decent job – white collar at that – selling insurance for the Prudential Company. This was a considerable step up from his pre-war occupation as a delivery boy for the Co-op.

Sue and I were the latest additions to a long line of Wingates. The family name existed in Britain long before the Norman invasion. Anglo-Saxon in origin, it probably goes back to the 5th or 6th century. It's a place-based family name, denoting the fact that our hardy ancestors lived in a windswept mountain pass or valley. Variously "Windgate", "Windegate" or even "Windeatt" it was passed through the generations and the centuries in evolving forms.

There was an original connection with the North of England – a family seat in the town of Wingate, in Kelloe parish in County Durham – as well as a thriving Scottish line. Whatever the starting point, the clan dispersed throughout the UK and well beyond. Some Wingates wandered as far as the new American colonies in the early 1700s, joining the hardy protestant settlers in Virginia. Others reached Australia.

A few achieved fame and distinguished office, like Sir Francis Reginald Wingate, who ascended to high levels in the British imperial administration, becoming Governor-General of the Sudan from 1899 to 1916 and High Commissioner of Egypt 1917-19. He lived to the ripe old age of ninety-two, dying three years after my birth.

Orde Wingate, son of Sir Francis' cousin, gained more public acclaim in World War Two, having founded, trained and led the daring Chindit guerrillas against Japanese forces in Burma. A driven, obsessive character, who some thought insane, he was reputedly one of the few people who could face down Winston Churchill. His early death in an air crash in 1944 added to his mystique. There was much controversy surrounding the strategic value of Wingate's long-range Chindits, but they were certainly of great public relations value. They enabled the war-time government to celebrate how British troops were matching the formidable Japanese for courage and endurance in fetid jungle conditions after the earlier humiliating defeats, which culminated in the surrender of Singapore.

Our scion of the Wingate line, not so closely related, couldn't boast of such derring-do, most of them coming from solid farm labouring stock. However, they did their own war time duty. They were clearly hard-working and respectable people, who had an elementary education and a desire to take advantage of the improving opportunities in post-war Britain.

My parents, being newly-wed as the war ended, had moved to St Ippolyts in 1946. At first, their situation was uncomfortable, particularly for my mother, because they stayed for two years with my father's parents in the small family council house, before they were allocated their own home. Regarded as being "stuck-up," because she came from London and spoke with a "posh" accent, my mother found the early years difficult and Dad's parents stern and distant. I suspect this was largely owing to their tough background bringing up eight children in poor circumstances, which made them unimpressed by a soft city girl. For her part my mother was shy, having had a sheltered upbringing, and lacked self-confidence. This reticence was interpreted, by the village folk, at first anyway, as arrogance. She, in turn, felt isolated and homesick in this quiet rural corner, and missed her family greatly.

Whilst she was struggling to learn the arts of housekeeping and motherhood, my father, in contrast, was attracting a reputation for himself as a sporting hero. Playing for local club Hitchin Town he became a local celebrity. When he had emerged from the army in early 1946, he was good enough to be offered professional terms by two clubs, Portsmouth and Notts County. However, he was already twenty-seven, and just married.

Professional footballers in those days received a statutory fixed wage of five pounds a week, which was not enough for an ambitious man with a growing family. Instead he opted for amateur status with Hitchin and this proved a sensible decision. Through contacts at the club he was offered the Prudential job, and his fame ensured a warm reception at many a Hitchin household when he knocked on the door to offer life insurance! Not only that, but the local coal merchant's presence on the Club's board meant we also received free coal – a priceless perk when this was your sole source of heating your home.

Frank Wingate, my father, and Freda Rule, my mother, had met on a tennis court somewhere in South London. He, dashing in his uniform, was a sergeant in the Signal Corps of the Herts and Beds Regiment, stationed in the area. She, attractive and cheerful was a laboratory assistant, testing insulin. It was in the early years of the war when they first met, but Frank kept coming back to see her, and she stayed loyal.

Bromley in south London, where Mum lived, was a dangerous place to be through the war years. The German bombers, heading for the centre of the city or the docklands, regularly passed overhead and unloaded their destructive cargoes. Later, the area endured the random attacks of the V1s, the "doodle bugs" or buzz bombs, and the V2s, their silent successors, which exploded with no warning.

As children we heard the tales of the family's miserable, long nights, sitting under the stairs, exhausted, waiting for the all-clear sirens. We were shocked by the story of the German bomb which smashed through the neighbour's roof and bored through the building to the cellar – then fortunately failed to explode. Once, when my father was staying with the family, sleeping on the landing beneath a window, a doodlebug exploded in the street below, blowing out the glass all over him. He was unscathed. Mum told us how you heard the flying bombs coming overhead, with their distinctive rhythmic drone, and how you leapt for the nearest cover if it stopped, for then you knew it was falling. She described how she and her sister had to scramble from their bicycles on one occasion as a buzz bomb cut out above them. They dived into a ditch at the roadside and the bomb exploded in a field across the road from their shelter, killing several cows.

She was not brave, my mother, but like many others she survived those times with a weary resignation. You thought not so much of the proximity of death as of your tiredness and the inconvenience of clambering out of bed in a hurry. The air raid siren had summoned you to the doubtful protection of the dank cupboard under the stairs. After these experiences, our village was a serene haven of peace and security. But perhaps a little uneventful also.

For my father, the war was an education and an awakening. Luckily, he never had to suffer the dangers of front-line fighting, being a signaller and generally deployed back in safer zones. But he travelled, to France, Belgium, Holland and Germany. He advanced his basic education. Above all he grew in self-confidence, comparing himself to others in the enforced democracy of the ranks, and climbing to the rank of sergeant. The village boy was outgrowing his village limitations.

But there was never any doubt he would come back. St Ippolyts was the best place on earth to live, it was certain. Here he already had status and a reputation. Having arrived at the age of eight with his parents in 1926, he took to village life without hesitation.

His family had escaped from grimy, industrial Nottingham, where my father was born. Exactly how the family landed on St Ippolyts is unclear, but it was motivated by the need to find work. Two or three years earlier, Dad's eldest brother, Reg, had first moved to St Ippolyts, because he found employment as a jobbing gardener in the area. Grandfather William had also been a gardener, and so followed on, finding work on the local estates. Initially, Dad's parents, Dad, his brothers Charlie and Ray, lived in a small, picturesque cottage in the hamlet of Gosmore at the western end of the parish.

Poor, but proud and respectable, the family was comprised of eight children altogether. Two of the older brothers, Dick and Cecil, remained in Nottingham, where they were already working and independent. While the male offspring generally prospered in their lives, the two girls were struck with tragedy. Lillian, the eldest girl, became pregnant while still single and had an illegitimate baby. As a result, she was banished to nearby Luton and ostracised. Though she lived barely ten miles away we never saw her. I never met my Aunt Lil and only understood her unkind treatment many years later. The other girl suffered an even worse fate. As a teenager she died of burns injuries when her nightdress caught fire in front of the household hearth. These family disasters were rarely alluded to and only then in the most discreet way.

Holding the family together through difficult times was my grandmother, Ellen, nee Hewer, who was the one who laid down the law and set the standards. Dad often told us, in teaching us how to present ourselves, how his mother had taught them the basic rules of personal hygiene.

"It doesn't matter how poor you are, you can still wash behind your ears, scrub your fingernails, polish your shoes and comb your hair," was the message passed on from Grandma Ellen. "And if you don't have any toothpaste, you can always use sand or salt (I never tried it!) and if you don't have any shoe polish, you have spit and elbow grease."

She could survive the relative poverty, for she had been born into worse in 1876. The daughter of a farm labourer from Poulton, Cirencester, she had found her way to Shab Hall, Sevenoaks, by the time she was twenty, to work as a housemaid. At this stately home, she met William Wingate, who was a gardener and groom on the same estate. Though he was three years younger, and apparently lied about his age on the marriage certificate to avoid the need for employer permission, the two were married in 1898. This was in the last months of Queen Victoria's reign, at Plaistow, Bromley, South London. They enjoyed some security of tenure presumably, until 1914, when the Great War began and cast its mournful shadow over the land.

The Wingate family, with several children, were also affected. But at least Grandfather William would be spared the horrors of the Flanders trenches, as he was too old to be conscripted into Kitchener's army. Instead he was sent to work in a munitions factory in Nottingham. This must have been a huge wrench for the family, which already included six children. Whilst the work would have been a drudgery, unhealthy and even dangerous, it afforded the family some security of income.

During this period, in Nottingham, my father, Frank, was born in September, 1918, just over a month before the armistice finally brought the bloodletting to an end. He came into a society that had been traumatised, shaken up and changed forever. The country was exhausted and a whole generation of young men had been decimated.

There would have been little work once the munitions factories were wound down, and jobs were hard to come by, especially with the returning soldiers expecting to be gainfully employed. So the post-war years were challenging, and even Ellen's resources stretched. But it was also a time of reconstruction and government promising a land "fit for heroes". A key part of this policy in the early 1920s was the Government's investment into hundreds of thousands of new council houses.

Dad's eldest brother Reg had moved back south by the mid-1920s, to St. Ippolyts, were he soon acquired one of these new homes and encouraged his parents to join him. And so my grandparents and father arrived in 1926.

Young Frank immediately settled in, as did the rest of the family. Attending the well-established parish school, under the auspices of the formidable headmaster Joey Cole, who had been there for twenty years, Dad progressed well, shining at sports and making friends in the village community. For his parents, who were designated one of the newly built council houses in the late 1920s, life must have seemed at least secure, if not prosperous. There was work, and there was a comfortable home of their own. The boys in the family, leaving school at fourteen, were becoming independent and contributing to the household.

On leaving school in 1932, Dad got his first job with the Co-operative Store in Hitchin, through his older brother Charlie. For the next seven years he lived a happy, if uneventful life, making a name for himself in local footballing circles.

He may have been destined to greater sporting triumphs if the Second World War had not broken out in September, 1939, the very month of his twenty-first birthday. In effect the prime years of his youth were thus stolen away. However, as he stayed unharmed he found the war years very liberating and they gave him a broader perspective and greater ambitions in life. He also met his future wife.

For my mother, the six years of conflict were, in contrast, limiting and rather bleak. But then, life hadn't been particularly kind beforehand anyway. The loss of her father when she was only nine years old was traumatic and her time at an orphan's school was so uninspiring that she could hardly remember anything about it.

Until her father died in 1932, family life was sweet, but the past had provided its share of tragedy for the Rules. Grandfather Frank (another one!) Rule, born in 1888 grew up in time to be sucked up by the Great War. His family, on the male side, had originated in Kent, while his mother came from Brighton. As her family name was Goldsmith, there is good reason to assume a strong Jewish background.

He married my grandmother Rosa in October 1914, just weeks after the war was declared. It was a fleeting experience of happiness for them before he was posted off with the Royal West Kents to Mesopotamia, modern- day Iraq, and an uncertain fate.

There he participated in the campaigns against the Turks, going to places and cities that were to become painfully familiar to British soldiers and their loved ones many years later ...... Basrah, Kut, Baghdad, Kirkuk, and Mosul. Censored cards and letters came from these distant towns. In one, kept and treasured by my aunt, my grandfather spoke longingly in 1919 of his wish to come home and expressed his love for Nanny. He writes of the misery of the Turkish prisoners he was guarding, and of the endless mud and flies. "Why can't we all just go home now?" he asks. He was away, without leave, from 1914 for five long years, but at least he survived. Scarred mentally and ill with malaria, he suffered, but he returned, unlike his brother Alf, who was shot through the neck by a sniper at the battle of Kut in 1916.

As our mother frequently pointed out, Nanny's lot in life was beset by hardship, which began even at her birth in

1891 in St Pancras. Her father, a British soldier, called Young, had married an Irish woman with the name of Murphy from Dublin. This in itself would have been very controversial at the time, as he was almost certainly based in Ireland as part the "occupying" military, keeping Ireland under control. There is no record of him on the English census records of the time. She, on the other hand, would have likely been ostracised by her community for marrying a British soldier.

Tragedy ensued, for, within a few years of her birth, Nanny's mother died of tuberculosis. She was packed off to a convent in Brighton, while her father moved on with her brother, and disappeared into the mists of time. There seems to be no further record or knowledge of him.

Nanny grew up then, parentless, in the convent, until leaving to go into domestic service, probably aged fourteen. At one stage she worked as a children's nanny to the then Lord Mayor of London, before meeting Frank Rule and enjoying a brief few years of contented family life until his untimely death.

For my mother then, meeting and marrying my father, lively and ambitious, must have seemed like a golden opportunity to escape the grey cycle of life in London. For him, my mother was an ideal partner – modest, well-spoken and naïve. As a city girl, she was quite a catch for this aspirational village boy, and definitely a cut above the country girls of his youthful flirtations. He would bring her back to his village with pride.

He was thirty-two and she was twenty-seven in 1950. The Wingates had arrived and were multiplying. They looked forward to a decade of steady improvement in living standards and continuous peace. As their prime minister was to tell them at the end of that ten years – they had "never had it so good".

Chapter Six
Posh, Common or Normal

Our next door neighbour, on the "upper" side, living in the first of a row of bungalows stretching along Waterdell Lane up to the bend in the road, opposite the allotments, was Mrs Ellis. She was old, small and round and always wore glasses, a smile and a floral pinafore. Most important of all, she spoiled us Wingate children, and invited us into her house to offer us a biscuit or a sweet. Mum said that it was good if we visited her, but I didn't think she was lonely, because, although she lived by herself, she seemed happy and smiled a lot.

Her house was always so clean and tidy, with everything put in its proper place. There were lots of photographs on the sideboard and shelves in the living room, which had a funny stale odour, and demanded to be treated with respect, like our front room. We had to be on our best behaviour at Mrs Ellis's, and make sure we wiped our feet when we went in. We didn't mind this. It was worth it, because she always gave us some tasty treat, and praised us for being good children.

Her son, Peter, was widely respected, because he had a very important job with British Rail. When he came to visit, which was about once a week, Mrs Ellis was very happy. Dad said he was extremely brainy and was editor of a

British Rail newspaper. I could see he was intelligent, because he wore thick black-rimmed reading glasses, had a full head of head, slicked back with Brylcreem, and always carried a briefcase, which was a sure sign of a professional. Goodness knows what high level papers and magazines he carried in that briefcase. He was always friendly to us neighbours, adults and children alike, but Mum and Dad didn't speak very long with him, beyond a greeting. He didn't talk to us much either, as he was probably too busy with important British Rail matters to bother with children.

The whole of Waterdell Lane, which ran from the main London Road leading to Hitchin, down to the village of Gosmore, had been built up before the war, with houses like ours or bungalows like Mrs Ellis's – perhaps forty or fifty dwellings. A further forty or so were put up along Mill Lane, which ran parallel to Waterdell Lane, at the other side of the recreation ground. These new houses accommodated the growing village population, as well as newcomers, giving a total population of about a thousand.

Most of the people living here were quite normal – like us. The Dads had ordinary jobs, like insurance agent, or dustman, or bus driver, mechanic and so on, while the Mums stayed at home to keep the house and the children clean, cook the food and iron the clothes. For example, my good friend, David Jenkins, had a normal family. His father, Roy, worked at Luton Airport, but I was never sure what he did there. I do know he wasn't a pilot, which was a pity, because that would have been more interesting. Mrs Jenkins was called Anne, and she was "an angel" according to Mum. Anne went to church regularly and helped everyone.

She was not as beautiful as my mother, and wore thick-rimmed glasses, but she was always cheerful and I very much liked going around to their house. Firstly, David and I could play football in their back yard, which was bigger than my lawn at home. Also, their house reeked of good cooking. Something was always stewing, boiling or frying on the stove or baking in the oven and Mrs Jenkins always had something delicious on offer. Inside the house was much untidier than ours, but very relaxing. I felt comfortable at the Jenkins' and didn't feel I had to be on my best behaviour. Furthermore, Anne Jenkins called me "Fantastic Frank", which made me feel very proud. Roy Jenkins had played football with Dad when they were at the village school. Dad said Roy, who was a redhead, was a passionate player but not that skilful. But David was a good footballer, and played with me in the school team, and that was one reason he was a close friend.

There were many families like this in our village, where the father had been a contemporary of my father and the son was now a similar age to me. "Tich" Breed, for example, the youngest of a family of six brothers, had a son called Philip, who was in my class. There were the Chalkleys, the Westons, Turners, Russells, Saiches and many others, most of whom had generations of history in the village.

But other people were different in some way. Next door to us, on the opposite side to Mrs Ellis, lived Mamie. She, my parents assured us, was posh but poor. Living entirely alone, she was a widow, with her only son Brian being away at boarding school. Mamie's husband had been a war hero, a Wing Commander, who died in action fighting for his country. This made me very curious and I would have liked to have asked her about her husband, but Mamie never spoke to us. I only rarely caught sight of her – a slender, well-dressed and carefully coiffured lady, living in the shadows.

It was hard to understand why she lived next door to us in a council house like everyone else, because people who talked like her normally lived in mansion houses, or in London. Dad explained to me that she had to live like this because she only had a small pension after her husband was killed. I found this very unfair, and felt very sorry for her, for the wife of a Royal Air Force war hero should surely have been given enough money for a big house. Mum and Dad liked having Mamie as a neighbour because she was "quiet and respectable", and we could have been very much unluckier.

If Mamie was poor, then the McMurtries were rich. They must have been, because they lived in the grandest house in the village, which was as big as a country home, with a huge garden, the size of a park, and driveways leading from the main road to the front door. They weren't as rich or as posh as the Queen or as the Bowes-Lyon family, who had "connections" in our part of Hertfordshire, but they were the aristocracy of our village. Obviously, we had nothing to do with them and hardly even saw them, except on "Bob-a-Job" week or at church occasionally. As a Cub Scout I had been to their house, timidly knocking on the door and asking if they needed any chores doing. A smart elderly lady came to the door and quickly summoned someone who seemed to be the gardener. She didn't really take much notice of us, but the gardener was very friendly and gave us a job weeding the paving in the garden.

Another time we found ourselves sitting in the row of pews directly behind the McMurtries in the church. I think it was a school event. Sitting behind them made us a little nervous as we had to behave as well as them and not giggle or play around. However, at a quiet point in the service, Mr McMurtrie suddenly farted loudly. That was enough to crease us up. I mean posh people farting like Jamie Shilton did deliberately was just hilarious. But then old man McMurtrie turned around to us. He was as red as a beetroot. He was surely going to scold us for laughing. Instead, however, he said: "I do beg your pardon," to us children, like we were adults. We just collapsed in giggles again and it was a struggle to get through the rest of the service without being thrown out of the church.

Other people were also slightly different, because of their education or background. Mr Sergeant, the head teacher of the primary school, commanded additional respect and deference from adults and children alike. He had to be especially clever and well-educated, probably at university, to be a headmaster and he always wore a dark blue pinstripe suit. We were in awe of him. He spoke in a deep loud voice like an army sergeant-major, ordering us to queue up, put our pens down, be quiet and so on, though he was kind as well and never caned anyone. He did have a cane and showed it to us sometimes as a deterrent, but he never used it, or not that I knew about.

Mr Livingstone, the class three teacher (we had four classes in our primary school) who took the eight and nine-year olds, was thin and had a shock of white hair. He was gentle and kind and wore a tweed jacket with leather patches on the elbows. He was also very brainy and produced plays with us, but I never understood why he supported Bury in the third division, because they were just a small town somewhere up north and never won anything, not like Luton, who had reached the FA Cup Final in 1959.

Other people were not at all posh or educated and they were quite common. The Wyndhams, who lived down the road, were like that, according to Dad. He said Mrs Wyndham had been the village bike, whatever that meant, but Mum, on the other hand, said she had a heart of gold. Dad said she shouldn't get too friendly. I thought Mrs Wyndham was really jolly. She was quite fat, had greasy hair, and wore a large grubby pinafore most of the time. She wore glasses and had red cheeks, probably from all the washing she did in the scullery for her large family. Fred Wyndham worked on the dustcarts, so he had to have blue overalls on. He never said anything, but Mrs Wyndham talked non-stop and laughed a lot. She always had apples or cake to give us when we went to their house.

I went there quite often because I was friends with Tony, who was about my age. Tony had three brothers. One was older, almost grown up, while Wiggy was about fourteen. I never knew why he was called Wiggy or what his real name was, because no-one ever asked. Tony also had a younger brother, Keith, who was a very good footballer. Although a year younger than me, he already played in the school team. Tony was no good at football at all, but he had a great collection of model cars and vehicles, including Dinky toys. We could play for hours, lying in the dirt of the flower beds and pretending to build roads and drive cars along them. Dad didn't really approve of this, because he didn't want me to be too friendly with Tony. Mum didn't like it because I always came back home extremely dirty after playing cars with Tony.

Some other people in the village were quite poor. You could see this, because their children, who came to our school, were scruffy. They had stains on their clothes, or they didn't comb their hair properly, or clean their shoes. Dad always told us that, however poor you are – and his family, with eight children, had been very poor – you can always take care of your appearance. Those people who were poor, who didn't keep themselves clean, were regarded as common.

You could also tell if people were posh or common by the way they spoke. Mamie, for example, spoke with an upper-class accent. This was definitely recognisable, but hard to identify. Something to do with the way vowels were pronounced and the precision of enunciation. Royalty and aristocrats, and those who had been to Oxford and Cambridge, as well as most politicians and BBC news reporters, spoke in this way. My parents were not expecting us to talk exactly like this, which was faintly ridiculous. "Lah-di-dah" they would call it, but they did not want us to speak "common" either. Consequently, we were often being corrected.

We were not supposed to drop our "aitches" for a start, which we often did. Our local town was, after all, not "Itchin Arts" but "Hitchin Herts". "Ain't" for "Haven't" and "Innit" for "Isn't it?" were frowned upon. "Pardon?" was preferred to "Wot?" School teachers, naturally, reinforced this piecemeal process of social betterment.

Some families were different from the normal villagers for other reasons. In Waterdell Lane, for example, the Skeggs owned their own home and were successful businessmen. They owned the only industrial enterprise in the village – an iron foundry. This was a great mystery to me. I passed it on my way to school and back every day, but never went inside the yard. It contained large sheds, like warehouses, and lorries came in and out continuously. Constant loud noises, like the clashing of metal banging against metal, the hissing of sparks like someone was welding, and engine sounds came from the interior. I guessed they were smelting scrap metal and producing iron bars, but I never discovered what was really happening there.

However, this made the Skeggs relatively wealthy and their house was probably the largest in Waterdell Lane. Nevertheless, they weren't snobbish at all and were well liked. Their son, Raymond, was a year of so older than me, so he wasn't a friend I played with. One day, everyone said, he would take over the iron foundry.

In addition to the foundry, shops, pubs and farms formed the backbone of commercial life. Tooley's, the general store in Gosmore, a mile away from our home, sold everything, from food to hardware and household goods. It was untidy and packed with products from floor to roof. Old Mrs Tooley knew where everything was. Sweets, vegetables, paint, towels, she had them all. Alderman's, however, in the other direction, which I could reach in five minutes if I ran, was my favourite. Mr Alderman's tiny premises were just a newsagent and sweet shop. Its beauty was the display of old-fashioned sweet jars on the counter. What a joy to take one's time on pocket money day, to look along that row of sugary delight in making one's selection. Gobstoppers, chews, lollies, humbugs, bulls eyes, liquorice all sorts, butterscotch, salted peanuts, fruit mix, bonbons, lucky bags, lemon sherbets – it was so hard to make the most of your sixpence pocket money.

My usual choice was two ounces of salted peanuts (threepence), one gobstopper (penny), two halfpenny chews (penny) and four farthing chews, preferably liquorice. On a good Saturday, this feast would last through to the evening, when we had shared family toffees. On a bad day, I could finish everything before getting home.

Mr Alderman was patient but not particularly friendly. I wonder how he made a living from this tiny business, with limited stock, in a small village. The largest shop in the village, a general store lying next to the main road to Hitchin, was also the Post Office. Mum didn't normally shop there, except to post letters or buy stamps.

There were plenty of pubs in our village and I also thought it surprising they survived. One of the oldest was the Bull, a timber framed building in the lower village of Gosmore. But there was the Bird in Hand, the Greyhound, on the main road, the Olive Branch, up in the old village, near the church, and Redcoats. Pubs were places for men to drink beer together and we were never allowed in. I understood decent women didn't go in either, as it wouldn't be proper. However, in the summer this changed, as families could go together in the long evenings to enjoy the pub gardens. Often, though, this was quite boring as once we had finished our lemonade and packet of crisps, we had to hang around until our parents emerged to take us home.

We lived in a rich farming area. Light, chalky soil covering the rolling hills of the Chilterns made for rewarding mixed farming and so we were surrounded by fields of crops and cows. These weren't over-wealthy or extensive estates but working family farms with down-to-earth owners. To us, farmers appeared quite wealthy, driving Land Rovers and riding horses around, and were apart from the village somehow. I didn't know much about farming, apart from occasional visits to my school friend Peter Dawson's farm. I couldn't really take to it though. I wasn't that interested in animals, and farming seemed to be quite cruel, like the way Peter told me about drowning the kittens in a bucket because they weren't needed. I thought they should try to find them a good home or sell them to a pet shop. It was also quite dirty and muddy in the farmyard with a smell of manure and cow shit, which was quite off-putting.

We didn't have any foreigners in our village, with one strange exception, which puzzled me. Working and living at the Skeggs' iron foundry was a German family. He was called Hans and his wife was called Ingrid. They had two children, much younger than me, who went to our primary school, but I didn't know them. I found it hard to understand why we allowed a German family to live here, when we had not long before had a war with Germany, in which many people, including some men from the village, had been killed. I was told by my parents that he had been a prisoner of war, and that the field near St Ibbs Park had been a prisoner of war camp. This was quite exciting to hear, but surely the prisoners wanted to go home when the war finished?

Apparently, Hans preferred to stay here because he had a good job at the foundry and Ingrid came from Germany to join him. I saw a lot of programmes on TV about the war and how cruel the Nazis had been. I could also see that the cities in Germany had been badly damaged and that Hans maybe didn't want to go back to that. Dad had been in the army in Germany at the end of the war, and he explained that there was terrible destruction. He felt sorry for the ordinary Germans and said they were led astray by Hitler.

Anne Jenkins, who was kind and wise about people, thought that Hans and Ingrid were good people and Christians and had nothing to do with the Nazis. Also, I knew about another German, Bert Trautman, who had been a prisoner of war too. As goalkeeper for Manchester City he played throughout the cup final with a broken neck and was a football hero, so not all Germans were that bad.

There were no other outsiders living in the village, but some black people had moved to nearby Hitchin. I had never seen them but people called them "Blackies" or "Darkies". My sister Sue, who was two years older than me, and went to the Girls' Grammar School in Hitchin, watched the news on TV a lot. She said that this was wrong and unkind and that black people should be called "Coloureds". They came to this country to work driving busses and being nurses and they had a right to do this because they had moved from the West Indies, which was part of the British Empire. However, none of them had settled in our village.

Other strangers passing through sometimes included gypsies and tramps, but they were treated with suspicion. Gypsy women, with their brightly-coloured clothes, would knock on the door sometimes, selling clothes pegs and tea towels. Mum would buy some things from them, mainly so they would go away, though she wanted to help them as well, because that was the way they earned some money. The way they made pegs, which were carved from whittled wood, split down the middle, was very clever, but otherwise we kept well out of the way. Sometimes they parked their caravans at the edge of the village, but then they left a mess, like old cars, and people wanted them to move on. We were curious about their camps, but didn't dare go too close, in case we were kidnapped. Usually they moved on after a few days.

Horace was another strange person in the village. Dressed in blue overalls and a cap, he was very tall and thin and had a long face, like a horse. As our village road sweeper, he spent all his time going up and down Waterdell Lane and other roads, pushing his green cart and carrying a huge brush and a long-handled shovel, sweeping up the leaves and muck and scooping them into his cart. He would stare at us children went we went by, smile and greet us. "Hallo, young Frank," he would say. Dad told us that Horace was "a bit simple" but quite harmless. I thought it was sad that he just spent all his time sweeping the road and that he didn't have a proper job like other men. It must have been boring.

On the other hand, he always seemed quite content and at least his job was easy and he was outdoors. He didn't get stressed like Dad when he had to do his paperwork in the front room. Perhaps it was good to have work like Horace – easy and simple and without worries. Everyone in the village knew Horace and was friendly to him. He was certainly not posh, but he wasn't really common either. Nor was he normal like us. But he was a part of our village.

It didn't really matter what kind of person you were, for everyone seemed to get on with each other in our village. I wasn't aware of fights between people, but perhaps I just didn't see them. I thought it was good to be a child there, or simple, like Horace, because life was peaceful and there were no real dangers. Sometimes I thought I didn't want to grow up, as adults had problems like jobs and money and houses and responsibilities to contend with. Apart from school work I didn't have to worry about anything important. Also, being in a village, it wasn't as crowded as Hitchin or London and there was plenty of space to play. Yes, posh or common, rich or poor, farmer or foundry owner, insurance agent or road sweeper, we were lucky to live there.

Chapter Seven
Church on the Hill

In 1070, just four years after William the Conqueror had subdued the forces of King Harold at Hastings and forced himself upon the Saxon kingdom, a young noblewoman was brought over from Normandy. Although only a vulnerable sixteen years old, she was, in the fashion of the time, ready to be married.

This bride-to-be, Judith de Lens, was of fine aristocratic stock – her father being Lambert the Second, Count of Lens, and her mother Adelaide of Normandy. The fact that Adelaide was the sister of Duke William meant that young Judith had particular value as a marriageable commodity in the realpolitik of royal diplomacy.

As part of William's pacification and reconciliation policy, Judith was duly betrothed and married off to Earl Waltheof of Huntingdon and Northumbria, one of the leading Saxon nobles, so forging a strong link between their respective houses. Waltheof, was, according to annals of the time, a man of imposing physical strength, but rather weak in character and easily influenced.

Nevertheless, we can assume their marriage was, by the standards of the day, successful, and Judith bore three children, who in their day were also to make valuable marriages. It would seem Judith's life was blessed with wealth and security.

But within a few years this contented domestic picture would be shattered. Waltheof allowed himself to be seduced into a plot against the indomitable William. Along with two other prominent Saxon lords, he hatched the so-called "Revolt of the Earls". It was the only and last major act of resistance against the Conqueror. Local armies were raised in the West Country and Midlands and defiant gestures made. The rebellion had been sparked by various disputes with William, who, at the time, was back in Normandy, and revolved around another marriage disagreement.

Waltheof, however, dithering, soon lost heart and confessed his role in the revolt to Archbishop Lanfranc. Within months William and his loyal lords had regained the initiative. They raised the fyrds – the local militias – and the rebels were defeated, captured or scattered, some escaping overseas. Walfheof was seized and held prisoner for more than a year.

Matters turned from bad to tragic for him and Judith, for she was hauled before her uncle and forced to give evidence against her husband. Because of this testimony, and perhaps because William was particularly vindictive against the man who had been "granted" his niece in marriage and then deceived him, William showed no mercy. While the two other earls suffered confiscation and imprisonment, Waltheof paid the ultimate price and was beheaded in 1076.

Uncle William then decreed that his, presumably distraught, niece should remarry, betrothing her to the Earl of Northumberland as a suitable match. But in a show of unusual defiance the young widow, by then only twenty-two years old, refused and fled back to Normandy. William promptly seized her extensive landholdings in England.

Fortunately for her, the Conqueror's wrath did not last too long. Two years later Judith was back in England, forgiven, still unmarried and back in possession of her holdings. She was also contrite and clearly guilty about the role she had played in her husband's untimely fate. As a pious Christian lady of means she felt obliged to display atonement for the betrayal of her husband. Like other wealthy people of the age she decided to found religious establishments, where holy servants could intercede with the Almighty, through prayer and good works, on behalf of her eternal soul.

To this end Judith made grants to found the Benedictine house, Elstow Abbey, in Bedfordshire, in 1078. She also supported the building of a church in Kempston, Bedfordshire. Furthermore, she provided for a new church in a picturesque spot two miles south of Hitchin, Hertfordshire.

Sited on a hill overlooking the main road to London, south of Hitchin, the Church was dedicated to Saint Hippolytus, the patron saint of horses. Why Judith chose this location or that saint we shall never know for sure. The situation had no special religious significance, but commanded a broad view over the surrounding Chilterns, was secluded and conducive to spiritual meditation. As for nominating the patron saint of horses, there is a tenuous link with the similarly named Chapel of Saint Hippolytus in nearby ancient Royston. That holy place was a kind of subterranean religious hideaway.

Simple in structure, the new church of St Hippolytus comprised a nave and a chancel. Only later, in 1320, were aisles and a tower added, and it was partially rebuilt and strengthened in the mid-eighteenth century. Then in 1840, fine tracery work from the windows of nearby ruined Minsden Chapel was scavenged, giving the church a look very much as it remains today.

Legend has it that the small church became a favourite with horsemen and knights, who would bring their steeds to the church to be blessed. It is said that the famous crusading Knights Templars were visitors before leaving on their epic travels to the Crusades, to receive holy endorsement for their mounts and themselves. Carved crosses still to be seen on the exterior stonework were supposedly engraved with their swords.

Whatever the truth behind these romantic stories, one thing is sure. The new church became the centre of the parish of St Ippolyts, encompassing the local hamlets of Gosmore and Langley, as well as the scattered local farms. A village sprang up around the church and a community was born.

The repentant Countess of Huntingdon, as Judith was also known, lived on quietly, most probably dying soon after 1087, sometime in her thirties. In one peaceful location in North Hertfordshire, she left a lasting legacy on account of her guilty conscience. It was a legacy that was to survive and evolve through more than nine centuries and flourishes to this day in village life.

Chapter Eight
Days of the Year

Village life had its peaceful, repetitive routines, with the progress of the seasons marked by ancient religious and historical traditions. Easter, Guy Fawkes Night and Christmas Day were dates of varying significance to the family.

For me the year began well, for after the delights of Christmas celebrations, when everyone else was feeling depressed about the long winter evenings still stretching ahead, I had my birthday to look forward to on January 18th.

We always celebrated birthdays in the family and it was common practice among all my friends to hold a party on the day. This inevitably caused great excitement for the host, who would not only be the centre of attention and temporarily very popular among classmates, but could also anticipate receiving many presents.

There were drawbacks. Class politics cast a shadow over the process of preparing the guest list in the first place. Inviting favourites was simple enough. But what about those who had invited you in the past, even though they didn't score highly on your socially desirable ratings list? Then there was the problem of girls. Did I really have to invite any? And the whole decision-making was further complicated by the intervention of my mother. She had ideas on who should be invited too, but on grown-up reasoning of those who ought to be invited – even though they weren't particularly friends of mine – because they were lonely or deserving.

This diplomatic wrangling would be resolved eventually, at the expense of extending the guest list up to ten or twelve, rather than the more desirable six to eight. My parents were understandably concerned at the thought of a dozen energetic, over-excited youngsters charging around our small house, being confined indoors on account of the frosty January gloom outside.

We wouldn't think of holding a party anywhere else but at home, although this naturally placed the burden of organisation on my mother. Food and drink had to be prepared; festive decorations bought; and games planned. The latter was important, otherwise the party would be very dull.

On a school day the event began as soon as possible after we had arrived home about four o'clock. Friends would mostly walk home with us and the most important and thrilling part of the whole party would begin immediately – opening the presents, all of which would be neatly wrapped in appropriate gaudy wrapping paper. Ripping open the gifts invariably resulted in great joy, feigned or otherwise, depending on the type of gift. Board games and books never went down very well with me, unless they involved a football theme. Toy weapons were popular, but I had a Tommy gun and a bow and arrow set already! Nevertheless, the present opening was enjoyable.

Usually we would then sit to have our birthday "tea", which would be colourful and generous enough to make sure our family reputation for parties couldn't be tarnished.

The table would groan with sandwiches and sweets. Ham, egg and jam sandwiches on white bread were the most favoured. If we were lucky, there were sausage rolls and cocktail sausages on sticks too. But the most sought after were the cakes and desserts. Homemade fairy cakes topped with icing disappeared quickly, as did the marsh mellows. Everyone saved space for the jelly, blancmange and ice cream, however, coming in various colours. These were sophisticated dishes for special occasions! All this washed down with lemonade and Tizer. It was really living.

A suitable finale for the enthusiastic eating was provided by the birthday cake, baked by Mum, smothered in icing and decorated with the requisite number of candles. I had to blow these out in one go in order to qualify for making a secretive birthday wish. Meanwhile, a discordant rendering of "Happy Birthday" would be screeched out by the assembled guests.

With barely time to digest the feast, consumed as though we were all malnourished, we launched into the party games, by now wearing our party hats. I found the messy and more embarrassing games the most entertaining. Apple dunking in a large bowl of water would amuse everyone as the victim tried to retrieve the floating apple with hands held behind the back. But even more fun was the flour game, in which the competitor had to locate and remove a sweet from under a small pile of flour, while using only his or her mouth and not using hands. It naturally finished with the victim's face covered in flour, as well as their clothes, the table and the surrounding floor.

We also had another slightly disgusting food game, whereby the victim, blindfolded, had to guess what they were tasting. With samples of tomato ketchup, brown sauce, mustard, sugar, pickles and salad dressing on offer, it wasn't pleasant, but generally applauded as hilarious, watching the unfortunate taster react in shock to the more extreme samplings.

As the party wore on and we became noisier, boisterous and red-faced, the games evolved into the more physical types. Blindman's Bluff could be quite raucous and deteriorated into a form of tag or even wrestling. Having around ten boys charging around our home was not Mum's idea of fun, and we had to be settled down. But by this time, perhaps six or seven o'clock it was, anyway, time to be thinking about going home.

The most dutiful parents would show up to take their offspring away home in the dark of the village lanes. Finally, those living nearby, or with less concerned parents, were gently ushered to the door. It was time for Mum to clear up the mess, while I continued, with party hat still firmly perched on my head, to sort through my presents, already deciding which ones I would discard. Then, finally, exhaustion would set in – red-faced exhaustion from the excitement and from playing the host. Tiredness from the games and from over-indulging. Time for bed. The party was over for another year, leaving some fast-fading memories of a special day.

Spring then dragged out uneventfully until Easter, bringing at least lighter evenings and milder weather. One notable date interrupting the benign advent of warmer months was Pancake Day. We were instructed at school that this was properly called Shrove Tuesday, on which day we should ask for forgiveness for our sins. For on the following day, Ash Wednesday, was the beginning of Lent when we should give up something – like sweets – for forty days. This replicated the time of self-denial and contemplation that Jesus spent in the desert.

However, the really arresting aspect of Shrove Tuesday, to existential children living in the moment, was the production of pancakes. This symbolised the final feasting on rich foods before the self-denials of Lent that were to follow. Mum and Dad had a lot of fun cooking the pancakes, which had to be tossed in the air to flip them over in the pan. Would they, or would they not, stick on the ceiling? They never did, but we enjoyed the possibility. We always had sweet pancakes, flavoured with jam or marmalade. They were delicious, and no less so that we weren't anticipating any sacrifices to follow in the coming weeks.

Easter usually arrived with unpredictable weather. It meant a school holiday and some awareness of the religious nature of the occasion. We were taught of the story of Jesus on the cross, his tribulations and death, and his subsequent resurrection. These tales of morality were drummed into us at school and at Sunday school.

At home, however, my parents not being religious, the Easter observance revolved more around chocolate. Easter eggs, in dark or milk or white chocolate, extravagantly and colourfully over-packaged were on sale in the shops for several weeks before the holiday. But the tradition was that children were not supposed to know what delights we could expect. The designated eggs were hidden in the household and we were not allowed to scoff them until Easter Sunday itself. Usually we located them, but didn't dare admit to this, in case we were denied the treat as a consequence. Thus we associated Easter with chocolate eggs – and rabbits – which featured heavily in retail marketing around this time. Ironic that the pagan symbols of fertility were more relevant to us than the Christian lore.

Easter sometimes meant visits to relatives, particularly to Auntie Brenda, my mother's twin sister, who lived in Bromley, which seemed a world away from our village. As a family we rarely went on trips together. It was probably considered too costly, or too difficult to manage. Not that we minded. None of our friends behaved otherwise.

One day trip we did enjoy, which we undertook several times at Easter, was to visit Dunstable Downs. These chalk ridges were the closest we had to any hills of any substance, and afforded wide views and open grassy walks. We would picnic there and, best of all, enjoy the sight of the gliders. For here the local gliding fraternity had optimal conditions as the warm thermals rising over the Downs lifted them gently higher to silently soar and sweep through the air. How brave they were to fly an aeroplane without an engine, I always thought; foolhardy but brave.

Summer weeks seemed to drift lazily by, with no special occasions to interrupt the endless feeling of wellbeing. Summers were sunny and hot – weren't they? Family holidays on the Norfolk coast created an idyllic retreat into irresponsibility with no timetables, classes or alarm clocks.

When they were done, however, and we were back to school, the inexorable advance of unwelcome dark evenings cast a shadow over September. Some relief came with Harvest Festival. This pagan festival, celebrating the conclusion of crop gathering and thanking the gods for their bounty (when they chose to afford it) at the autumn equinox had been tidily co-opted by the Church of England.

I found the services colourful and optimistic and somehow, more grounded, than other church rituals. Our village church would be bedecked in harvest offerings of all kinds – wheat sheaves from the farms; vegetables like large marrows and cabbage and potatoes from peoples' allotments; resplendent bouquets of flowers from gardens; cakes and pies and many assorted goods.

It seemed to us, shepherded to the church for special services from the school across the road, an Aladdin's cave of plenty and richness – a spectacular display of the plentiful nourishment we enjoyed in our rich and lucky country. Of course, the service reminded us of our good fortune and assured us that the offerings would be donated to the poor and hungry. This was eminently sensible, though I never knew which poor and hungry the food went to. It just disappeared. Did it go to the hungry in Africa? Or to the poor in England? But we didn't have any poor in England, surely?

My parents weren't interested in the religious ceremony, but approved of the sentiment. So Mum could be conjoined into baking a cake to provide my donation, though I think in past years, when busy, she had bought one. However, it was enough to appease my conscience as a good Christian, that I had done my part to feed the deserving. Also, I was glad that my contribution had been genuine and not tins of baked beans or fruit, which I knew some classmates has given in, and which didn't seem very Christian to me, though tins of food of course, did last a long time and would survive a journey to Africa.

Much less positive for the soul, but infinitely more fun than Harvest Festival, was the next major date on the annual calendar. As October brought dropping temperatures, cold nights and mists, and clocks turned back to lengthen the evenings, we had the spectacular excitement of Guy Fawkes Night to look forward to. Not only to anticipate, but to prepare for. Our creative inner selves were called into action.

Several weeks before the explosive event, we had to prepare our Guy. This was our way of playing a direct part in the celebration of Guy Fawkes' failed attempt to blow up the Houses of Parliament. We were taught about this at school and shown how the dastardly Catholics were attempting not only to subvert the glorious onward march of the Church of England and British democracy, but had the audacity to attempt to assassinate the monarch and the Lords who ruled us.

We would now share in the historic marking of this treacherous plot by burning the villain in effigy. This had resonance with an eleven-year old boy, for whom gore and war held a degree of fascination. But the more immediate and practical role of the dummy was to help us raise money to buy fireworks.

The first task was to prepare the Guy itself. Discarded shirt and long trousers were required. Do up all the buttons on the shirt, fasten the closed sleeve endings with string. Attach the shirt to the trousers – might need mothers' help here with some crude sewing. Then stuff the figure with straw or newspaper or both until it vaguely resembled the human form. Fasten the ends of the trouser legs with string.

A plastic bag, similarly stuffed with straw, would do for the head. It would have a very simplistic face drawn on it before being attached to the top of the shirt and adorned with an old hat. And there it was – not so much a cultural or artistic achievement as a shortcut to convincing innocent passers-by to subsidise our pyrotechnic ambitions.

To do this our Guy would be transported on one of my friend's trolleys from busy pedestrian spot to other crowded areas (relative to our sleepy village). Trolleys were prized possessions for boys my age. Usually made from discarded soap boxes and old pram wheels they provided much fun racing around, being pulled or pushed with one or two passengers. Manufacturing trolleys depended on your father's DIY skills or your own ingenuity. My father didn't have those skills, nor did I, so I usually shared with Tony Whitman from down the road.

Thus would we sit patiently at bus stops or outside the local newsagents, crying confidently "Penny for the Guy!" expecting to be rewarded for our hurried and scruffy efforts at dummy design. There was, of course, competition from other lads and girls, and the pickings were, to say the least, meagre. However, we persisted. Our parents were loath to waste money on potentially dangerous and disruptive playthings as fireworks, so this was our only hope for independent purchase.

We would indeed collect a few pennies here and there as good-hearted villagers entered into the spirit of the occasion. As soon as we had a few, we would organise a bus trip to Hitchin, our local town, where we would buy our fireworks. No-one prevented us. Bangers, our favourite firework, loud and startling and easily thrown, were only a penny each. Jumping Jacks, even more alarming to victims, caused greater disarray because of their unpredictability of movement. They cost threepence, however. Grander versions, like Roman Candles, were spectacular, but more expensive and decorative rather than lending themselves to mischief. Sparklers were cheap, but for the young ones.

Naturally, none of us could quite preserve the self-discipline to save all our weapons for the night itself and a good number would be tossed towards rivals or set off behind unsuspecting groups in the recreation ground.

Meanwhile, as November 5th drew nearer, a great spectacle was taking shape at the bottom of the village recreation ground. A bonfire, of dramatic proportions, was being built up by the men of the village for the communal festivity. Huge logs, wooden pallets, old packing crates, newspapers and other detritus were piling up and promising a conflagration to send flames and glowing embers high into the dark night sky.

On the night itself, which was invariably bitterly cold, misty and pitch black, the early evening fun would start at home, in the garden. Dad would have made a small bonfire and purchased a few tame fireworks. This was enjoyable, but I was outgrowing it and whilst I appreciated the colours and sounds of family explosives, I could hear from the rec the rumble of the gathering crowd and was impatient to join them before the huge bonfire was lit.

Finally, at about seven p.m., Dad, my sister Sue and younger brother Geoff, would walk out the back garden gate and down the few hundred yards of the playing field to the main event. A village Guy, properly made and looking, I thought, just like a real human, was perched above the fire, which was then lit to signal the start. It seemed like hundreds of people were there. Everyone was well wrapped up in duffel coats, gloves and scarves, their faces glinting ghoulishly in the light of the fire. The bonfire itself was mesmerising, crackling and roaring, splintering and spitting sparks into the blackness. Again and again we were warned not to approach. Again and again we edged nearer to feel the heat and see more closely the destructive dancing flames.

As well as the fascination of the fire we were treated to a grand pyrotechnic display. Huge rockets screamed into the sky and exploded, scattering into multicoloured showers. Giant roman candles that lasted for ever and whizzing Catherine wheels. This celebration of the foiling of treason went on for at least an hour. Meanwhile, the boys my age played mischief, throwing bangers into the fire, or behind unsuspecting groups of girls or dropping jumping jacks behind innocent families.

Towards the end, as the fire subsided, the great logs collapsed and the blackened newspapers shreds floated into the air. The Guy was reduced to ashes, and we ate baked potatoes, cooked in the embers. Everything smelt of cordite and ashes as we wended our way home, our senses overloaded, our ears humming and the freezing night overcoming the warmth of the occasion.

Once the charred remains had been swept up, Guy Fawkes Night was soon forgotten, the only trace being the burnt circle in the grass at the bottom of the rec.

November was a long and dreary month – foggy and gloomy. But once it came to an end we could at least start anticipating Christmas. It wasn't evident or so commercial, in the shops or on TV, until a week or so into December, when we would be reminded at school that nativity plays had to be rehearsed and crypts laid out. The story of Mary and Joseph at the inn; the miraculous birth; the wise men following the star, bringing gold, frankincense and myrrh; the shepherds watching their flocks by night. This tale had been well drummed into us. It was truly moving, though parts of it remained a mystery. I didn't get the virgin birth, nor did Mum and Dad, and I always wondered what those exotic gifts of frankincense and myrrh actually were. Nevertheless, the rituals were followed and were comforting. I liked singing the hymns and appearing in the school nativity play, though disappointed at only being a shepherd.

At home preparations began in earnest only a week or two before the big day. It was apparent that, whilst they looked forward to a break, the whole affair was a trying process for my parents, but they played their role with enthusiasm for us children.

Christmas decorations for the home were mainly self-made. Paper chains, consisting of interlocking rings of coloured paper, made from strips three of four inches long with ends glued together, were strung from each corner of the living room to the opposite one diagonally. Bright coloured paper sellotaped along the curtain rails on the top of the windows and tinsel above the fireplace.

Centrepiece was the tree – a natural fir tree that Dad somehow conjured up from the countryside, or did he just buy it? Placed in a plastic bucket of earth, concealed in decorative paper, it would be liberally adorned with tinsel, baubles and paper stars, which had been kept in a cardboard box in the sideboard since the previous year.

Then came the challenging part – buying Christmas presents for the family. I did save up some pocket money, but usually had to scrounge some extra from Dad to make sure I had enough for him, Mum, sister Sue and brother Geoff. It was best to do this disagreeable shopping just a day or two before Christmas and I considered Woolworths in Hitchin to be the ideal store. For there I could find something for everybody and it didn't cost too much. Aftershave for Dad usually went down well, so Old Spice was a favourite. For Mum a simple bracelet or broach because she liked anything I bought her. Sue was trickier, being more demanding, but a sensible hair brush would be appreciated. Geoff liked painting and drawing, so he was straightforward. A painting brush set or an artist pad would keep him happy. This had to be kept intensely secret, as the presents were smuggled in and wrapped, away from prying eyes.

While we youngsters fussed about presents, Mum and Dad were laying in provisions for family and visitors alike. Normally, we had no alcohol in the house, apart from the occasional bottle of stout, but for the festive season they bought whisky, sherry, Bristol Cream, Advocaat and even Benedictine liqueur. As well as the staples for the main meals – chicken, ham, sausage meat, stuffing and mounds of vegetables – most exciting would be the exotic extras we rarely had, such as nuts and dates.

Christmas Eve was unbearably tense. Carols on the radio. Carol services on TV and carol singers outside. Embarrassing but give them something for their efforts and they will go away, like the gypsy women selling clothes pegs. Later than usual, finally forced to bed. Pillow cases carefully set at the bottom of the bed. It was difficult to sleep.

I no longer believed in Santa Claus. I fully understood it was a lovely myth for small children, but I had outgrown it. However, this did not reduce the delirious anticipation about what I would find in the pillow case at the bottom of my bed. Exactly how Mum and Dad filled them in the night I didn't know, but I couldn't stay awake all night.

It was still silent and very dark when I awoke. The house was frozen in icy anticipation. Had they been yet? I would turn on the light and wake my brother, scramble to the pillow case. Oh joy! It was full of good things and on top, the leather football I had hoped for!

Now my sister and I, and Geoff, emptying our treasure trove on the floor would rush to our parents' bedroom to thank them. Near comatose after staying up late preparing everything, they would be pleased with our happiness, but order us to get dressed and go downstairs to play with our new toys in the living room. I was only six o'clock and they would follow soon.

It was bitterly cold and still dark, but we didn't notice. Wearing pyjamas and dressing gowns we would play contentedly on the carpet. What joy to have new annuals (especially about football), board games, toy cars and Airfix kits. As well as our presents, the pillow cases had been stuffed with sweets, nuts and fruit, the first of which we were soon devouring.

The entire day was a drawn out feast of self-indulgence. Once our parents were up and the fire in the grate was roaring, we began with a fried breakfast. By two in the afternoon we were tucking into a traditional lunch, with chicken and all the trimmings. For dessert we enjoyed the cloying Christmas pudding which had matured in the pantry over the previous few months. It would be lit with brandy first, then the squabbles erupted over who would get the threepenny piece hidden inside. Be careful not to choke on it!

Afterwards, following the Queen's speech on our unreliable black and while TV, we sank into a soporific afternoon and evening, fitfully playing with new possessions, and eating, always eating something. Chocolates to pick at, nuts to crack, fruits to peel and suck. The TV, constantly murmuring in the background, like the extra family member, singing carols, presenting entertainments and classic films. Was it *White Christmas* this year with Bing Crosby, or was it James Stewart experiencing miracles? Or was it Scrooge being terrified back into humanity. The images merged into a comfortable haze of plenty, satisfaction and over-consumption.

Boxing Day was clearer, soberer, less giddy, but still a part of Christmas. We may have visitors this day, and that was welcome because they would bring additional gifts for us. Relatives didn't necessarily choose the best presents, for clothes and books weren't ranked highly, but we enjoyed the anticipation of tearing open the colourful wrapping.

Uncle Ray, Dad's brother, and Auntie Pearl, usually came on Boxing Day. They were part of the tapestry of Christmas, like the Wise Men or the shepherds. Ray was inevitably cheerful, joking, cursing frequently and laughing loudly. I liked him, and Auntie Pearl too, who was elegant and sophisticated, with her coiffured hair piled high, red lipstick, horn-rimmed glasses and musky perfume. She spoke in a soft Scottish accent and worked in a drapery shop in Hitchin. The adults would sit in the front room in the afternoon, playing cards, drinking and talking. They always talked non-stop. I couldn't imagine what they were talking about for so long.

The days after were anti-climactic. The weather became even colder but clearer. All too soon the magical time of Christmas was over, giving way to frost and ice. Decorations were taken down and stored in the cardboard box for next year. Our tree was uprooted from its bucket and planted in the garden. All traces of the festivity were cleansed away.

But I did have my new leather football. A real one, with a nozzle and lacing. And I had an Airfix kit Spitfire to build. And an FA annual, season 1959–60, to read again and again. And I had my birthday in January to look forward to. Life was good, very good.

Chapter Nine
Hosting Henry

Our village was nearly the death of one of England's most formidable kings, whose untimely end would no doubt have changed the entire course of the country's history. Henry the Eighth, famous for breaking away from the Catholic Church, and for having those six wives, stayed frequently in the 1520s at the small manor house of Maydencroft in the parish of St Ippolyts.

This late medieval open hall house, simple in design, was owned by the manor of nearby Hitchin, which estate was, in turn, owned by Henry. He had inherited it from his grandmother Margaret in 1509. Presumably, Henry, by the 1520s in his thirties, sought peace and respite from the irritating affairs of state in this secluded spot.

Particularly frustrating was the state of his marriage to Katherine of Aragon, his first wife. Accommodating and dutiful as she was, Katherine had failed in her prime duty as Queen. She had been unable to produce a son and heir. Despite numerous pregnancies, miscarriages and stillbirths, she had only delivered a girl, and this spelt trouble for the new Tudor monarchy. It was essential to have a healthy, growing male heir to secure the succession and give confidence to the newly established dynasty.

He began to lose interest in Katherine and by 1524 had stopped sleeping with her. Just to complicate matters, a certain Anne Boleyn had joined the court in 1522 and was exciting Henry's attention. She was keeping him at arms' length, not wishing to become just another royal mistress.

No wonder he just wanted to get away, and what better sanctuary than St Ippolyts, just 30 miles to the north of London. Here he could indulge in his favourite pastimes of hunting and hawking undisturbed. He was at that time still an athletic man in his prime. He hadn't yet ballooned into the stout figure of later years captured by Holbein. Renowned for his ability to hunt from dawn to dusk, he revelled in the chase.

In nearby Hitchin he also practised archery, shooting on the fields called Butts Close named after the butts or targets. The open space is still there today as a town facility. In fact, Henry had made a point of forbidding the people to indulge in other wasteful pastimes, such as tennis, cards and shove groat (shove halfpenny). These idle pursuits were distracting the sturdy yeomen from sharpening their archery skills, so essential for the military effectiveness of local trainbands and therefore the King's armies when he needed them.

At Maydencroft he spent most of his time indulging in hawking. The use of trained hawks or falcons to catch birds and small animals was a popular sport in Tudor times, permeating all layers of society. It was mainly practised in the winter, when the need to replenish herds and the hard ground made the hunting of deer impractical.

A strict hierarchy of the birds was followed in hawking, with a king or noble, for example, keeping an eagle perhaps, while a poor commoner would have to make do with a kestrel. For the nobility a noble bird carried on the forearm was a classy accessory.

One Tudor aristocrat left us in no doubt as to his priorities:

"By God's Body I would rather that my son should hang than study literature. It behoves the sons of gentlemen to blow horn calls correctly, to hunt skilfully, to train a hawk well and carry it elegantly. But the study of literature should be left to clodhoppers."

In pursuing his obsession for hawking over-exuberantly in 1525, while residing at Maydencroft, Henry nearly paid with his life. But two years earlier he had already narrowly escaped death at the manor.

The chronicler Hall tells us that in the 14th year of his reign on October 15, 1523: "the Kyng's lodgying was on fyer and he in greate feare escaped."

Apparently he barely made it with just the shirt on his back.

Henry seems to have been accident prone – or was he just reckless – around this time, for in 1524, he shocked his retinue when taking part in a jousting contest. He failed to fasten his helmet correctly and was struck on the head by his opponent's lance. Somehow he survived with bad bruising.

In 1525, he was back in St Ippolyts. One day when chasing his hawk he was either distracted or showing off his regal athleticism, when vaulting over a ditch. Disaster struck. The chronicler Hall took up the story: "the Kynge following of his Hawke, lept over a diche beside Hychyn with a polle, and the polle brake, so that if one Edmond Moody a footman had not lept into the water and lift up his head, which was faste in the clay, he had been drowned; but God of his goodnesse preserved him.

So, fortunately for the unconscious Henry, a quick-witted servant saved him from an undignified end in a water-logged village ditch.

Historical "what-ifs?" are generally pointless, but some speculation as to the country's fate had not Edmond Moody saved Henry is entertaining. If he had succumbed to the mud on that day, the great religious schism that rent the church apart in England might never have happened. England would also have been deprived of one of its iconic kings and queens, his daughter Elizabeth.

As it was, Henry was by 1526 bewitched by Anne Boleyn. He seems to have stopped his flying trips to Maydencroft. By 1531, he was recognised as Head of the Church of England and by 1533, he officially divorced Katherine. Like a rumbling earthquake, the Reformation in England gathered momentum. Henry had unleashed a movement of historic proportion.

St Ippolyts continued its sleepy rural routines, though was later swept by protestant fervour. The manor of Hitchin, including Maydencroft, was given to Trinity College, Cambridge, in 1539. Mr Edmond Moody, meanwhile, was rewarded for his life-saving attention to duty with a lifetime pension of a groat a day.

My maternal grandfather, Frank Rule, served in
Mesopotamia in the First World War

Grandad Frank Rule

My maternal grandmother, Rosa Frances Rule, who
encountered much hardship in her life

...ium, transitius, by
of William Jolly; *b.*
1; educ. at Walnsey
ter; was subsequently
for the Co-operative
pecial Reserve of the
lled up on the outbreak
erved with the Expedi-
: and Flanders from 19
eded to Salonika, and
while on active service.

Light Infantry; served
ounds received in action

48, 2nd King Edward's
nybrook House, Santry,
now (1918) serving with
the late Major William
melton, co. Donegal, 26
llege, Dublin; intended
antime, he joined King
tionary Force in France
: 1st Canadian Mounted
g, from wounds received
toad. His Commanding
ce, and I always found
it of the ' slacker ' about
d his admiration for it,"
the most manly fellows

attn. Royal West Surrey
n action near Fleurbaix

Herbert Ruff, of Tindon Farm, near Worthing; served with the Expeditionary
Force in France; killed in action at Richebourg l'Avoué 9 May, 1915.

RUGG, ROBERT HENRY, Private, No. 6079 Middlesex Regt.; served with
the Expeditionary Force; died 25 Sept. 1914, of wounds; *m.*

RULE, ALFRED, Private, No. 1976, 1/5th Battn. The Queen's Own (Royal
West Kent Regt.) (T.F.), 2nd *s.* of George Rule, of 12, Shaftesbury Road, Beckenham, co. Kent, Horticulturist, by his wife, Elizabeth A., dau. of Elizabeth (and
George) Goldsmith, of Brighton; *b.* Beckenham, co. Kent, 25 Sept. 1886; educ.
Albemarle College there, and Clark's C. S. College; prior to the war was in the
Civil Service, and for some years in the 12th Territorial Battn. Middlesex Regt.;
later in the Civil Service Rifles, from which he resigned; when war broke out
he joined, 8 Aug. 1914, the 5th Territorial Battn. of The Queen's Own, and
volunteered for active service; went with his battalion to Jhand, India, about
the end of Oct. 1914, and from there with a small contingent to the Persian Gulf;
was present with General Townshend's Force during the retirement on Kut, and
for five weeks was with the besieged garrison; killed in action at Kut 13 Jan. 1916.
Buried in the English Cemetery there. His Captain wrote to his father: " Your
son is the first man of this battalion to be killed in action in this war." A com-
rade: " We were in the first line of trenches early one morning, and he was as
cheerful as ever, and was saying he wondered when they would be relieved;
the order was given to get blankets folded and be ready to move back into
second line for a rest; he stood up to fold his blanket, and at that moment
received a bullet in the back of his neck, being killed at once." His brother was
serving at the time in the same battalion in Mesopotamia; *wum.*

RULER, HERBERT JOHN, Private, No. 9752, 1st Battn. East Kent Regt.,
s. of Herbert Ruler, of Barming; served with the Expeditionary Force; died
at Bailleul 26 Oct. 1914, of wounds.

RUMBY, CHARLES, Sergt., No. 5640, 1st Battn. East Kent Regt.; served
with the Expeditionary Force; died at Bailleul 24 Oct. 1914, of wounds; *m.*

The death notice for great uncle Alf, killed by a sniper in
WWI in Kut, Mesopotamia

My father (with ball) aged 14, captaining the school team,
overseen by long-serving teacher Joey Cole. Left, middle
row, is Alfie Turner, who was to die in a Japanese prison
camp

My father in football and service uniform (left, with friend) during WW2

My mother, Freda Mary Rule, in her late teens, in London
during the war

The handsome couple. My parents' wedding, 1946

Dad, me and older sister Sue in front of our village
council house home, Waterdell Lane

Our family trying to enjoy the Prudential's annual Star
Dinner, around 1954. My sister's just spilt the soup in her
lap

Growing family. Younger brother Geoff has joined us

Country dancing in the village hall, circa 1960. I'm leading the pack with my hot date Patsy Sawyer.

Dad (head of table, far end) with his Prudential agents, circa mid 1960s

My mother and father, with brother Geoff and younger sister Sally, on holiday on the windswept Norfolk Coast. By then my sister and I were going our own way in the summer

St Ippolyts Church with war memorial, and school in the background.

The author in the porch of the 11th century village church,
2016

St Ippolyts primary school, today, showing the original
flint building built in the 1840s

Maydencroft Manor, where Henry the Eighth very nearly perished, is now a modern business centre

Chapter Ten
Charlie and Brenda

It was tradition. A family habit. On most Sunday afternoons my parents and we three children would visit Uncle Charlie in Stevenage. It was just a part of life, of the rhythm of the week, like getting up each day to go to school or watching *Popeye* on the TV on Monday nights.

Charlie was the fourth brother among the six Wingate boys. Dad was the youngest – the baby, the handsome one and the star footballer. Charlie was probably his favourite brother and the one he was closest to. This was likely because Charlie had played a role in bringing him up. In a family with eight children in the hard days of their growing up older brothers did that.

He was also favoured, however, on account of his proximity in age and his character. Confident, gregarious and good-humoured, with a rugged face, bulbous nose and gravelly voice, he was the life and soul of the party. A "ladies' man" when he was younger, he made the women laugh by slapping them on the bottom, which he did with Mum (and she didn't seem to mind). Despite this reputation, which he seemed to enjoy, he had finished up with plain, sweet natured, skinny Auntie Eva as his wife. Unlike the glamorous ladies with whom he had reputedly flirted in his younger days, Auntie Eva was unpainted, flat-chested and wore glasses and a frilly apron. But she had a kind of aura and everyone agreed she was saintly. She was softly spoken, forever busy and attentive to us all. Charlie adored her.

He was a milkman, an early riser who worked strange and long hours. He got up when it was still dark most of the year, which was somehow creepy. However, through his character and charm, Charlie had developed beyond being an ordinary milkman. He had progressed through the ranks and had become the manager of the local milk depot. A person of status, he was well-known in the community from the days of his delivery rounds and popular on account of his genial nature. Strangers greeted him warmly in the street.

Uncle Charlie was a tease, but I put up with him anyway. He called me "Frankie Boy" and tousled my hair, but he was funny and their house was always welcoming and informal. We didn't feel we had to affect our best behaviour, for it was just like being at home.

We would drive the three or four miles through the narrow, winding country lanes, bordered with hedgerows, to old Stevenage, where they lived. This enabled us to avoid the busy main roads and to bypass Stevenage New Town, the sprawling post-war settlement built for London overspill. It had a reputation for being rough and tough and genuine local people, like the old Stevenage folk, looked down on the johnny-come-latelys from London's east end, who dropped their aitches, used four letter words frequently and were likely to be criminals.

Charlie's was a terraced council house about the same size as ours, with a small conservatory at the back and narrow garden. To me it appeared cramped and confined, and a little spartan, but cosy and comfortable. As at home, daily life was conducted in the living/dining room, where the coal fire crackled on endlessly, while the front room, facing the street, lay bare and neglected.

Both families, the five of us, Charlie, Eva and their son David, who was two years older than me, would crowd together, round the dining table and fireside to have "tea" together, often perching our plates on our knees.

Sunday tea was invariably salad. A couple of lettuce leaves, a tomato, cut in half, with cucumber slices, and a slice of ham or oxtail, all served separately on the plate, with a blob of Heinz salad cream on the side for flavouring. There may be tinned crab and beetroot as well and sometimes pork pie. It was not always very filling for my taste, but piles of bread and butter helped make up the shortfall. Cakes, baked by Auntie Eva, and biscuits were plentiful too, along with an endless supply of tea. Auntie Eva's tea was always made in the teapot and was black, strong and bitter, requiring a lot of milk and sugar.

When the meal was over the young ones would decamp to the front room. Though chilly in winter, this held a great attraction, because cousin David kept his amazing collection of comics there. Hundreds of them were piled precariously on shelves, on the sofa and on the floor. There were war comics, my favourite, as well as superhero comics. Superman, Batman, Spiderman, the Hulk, and many other wondrous characters, performed their stupendous deeds in that bleak front room and transformed it into an action-packed world where good fought bad in its universal manifestations.

Many a happy hour would be spent, lounging on the sofa or sprawled on the carpet, reading how the brave Tommies had defeated the cruel and unintelligent Germans or the inscrutable, suicidal Japanese, or how Superman had, at the very last moment, yet again saved the world from destruction.

We learnt from these comics how the British held the moral high ground. Our soldiers were always considerate and heroic, whereas the Germans could only say things like "Englische Schweinhund", "Mein Gott" or "Kaput" and behaved abominably. As for the Japanese, they attacked in suicidal waves, shouting "Banzai" and giving their lives cheaply for the Emperor. This is how we took our first steps into studying history and understanding intercultural relations.

Rosy cheeked, affable cousin David, tolerating his younger relatives, also transfixed us with his guitar playing. As none of us were musical, he was truly to be admired, as he strummed the few chords he knew. His ambition was to be a pop star and this was indeed a glittering ambition, though I had little time for such girlish matters as pop music, and especially love songs, at that time.

As we had been told in hushed tones, David had been adopted by Charlie and Eva. His mother, my aunt Anne, married to Dad's oldest brother, Dick, had tragically died in childbirth. As Dick was unable to bring up a baby, the family agreed that Charlie and Eva would take over and this became the natural order of things. As Dick was much older, and lived in Nottingham, we saw very little of him and as far as David was concerned, Charlie was "Dad."

Charlie and Eva also had a son themselves. This was Stephen, who was just a year older than me. However, we never saw so much of him. He was often out or upstairs when we visited and he kept himself to himself. Although a loner, he was not unfriendly, but we never got to know him as we did David.

In the summer, we could go outdoors to the local playing field across the road. The grown-ups would adjourn to the nearest pub for the early evening, while I went with David over to the makeshift football pitch. Whole groups of boys would play, teams of up to ten or fifteen, of ages varying from eight to fifteen, competing on an extensive field, with jacket and sweaters on the ground to mark out the goals.

Here I was in my element, for I loved the competition and physical roughness of it all, and I had inherited some of my father's skill. Football brought me recognition.

Eventually, the evening would draw in. We would be summoned back to Charlie's and packed in the uncomfortable green van for the journey home. It was without exception a most miserable time, for it led ineluctably to washing, bedtime and the prospect of school on Monday.

As Charlie was the closest confidante for my father, so Auntie Brenda was for my mother. Not surprising, for they were twins and true soul mates. Not a week passed without Mum trekking around the mile of Waterdell Lane to the London Road crossroads, where the nearest public phone box was, to catch a few minutes hurried conversation with Brenda.

They hadn't enjoyed the easiest of lives. Until they were eight years old, life was reasonable, for their father, also Frank, was a middle ranking civil servant. In the 1930s this meant considerable status and a secure income. Mum always told us proudly that Grandad worked "in central London in a big office". However, tragedy struck when he contracted cancer and died quite quickly. Mum always claimed it was a result of his wretched time in World War

One, when he had suffered the privations endured by so many of his fellow soldiers.

She told us spine-chilling tales of the cancer eating away his face and how the primitive radiography ("they stuck needles into his face and it just spread") made matters worse.

The death of her father pulled the rug from under the family. Now there was no income. Nor was there a welfare state to rely on. Her mother, Nanny to us, had to go into service, becoming a domestic servant. The girls were found a place in a dreary girls' boarding school, in which they languished until fifteen years old. However, as Mum frequently pointed out, they considered themselves lucky, because their mother's connection to the Mayor of London himself had helped secure them their places at this charitable establishment. The alternative would have been destitution. Mum's brothers, one older, one younger, were also sent to boarding schools.

When they finally emerged from the school, they re-joined their mother in South London, in straitened circumstances. Both got jobs at Boroughs and Welcome doing tedious laboratory work related to insulin. Life might have started to improve but then the Second World War broke out. In 1939, they were just sixteen, so the joys of teenage life that other generations came to expect passed them by and life was monotonous and precarious in South London, in those cheerless war years.

No wonder that the twins were close. And no wonder that we visited Auntie Brenda when we could. This was usually at Easter time. Sometimes she and her family had come to visit us in St Ippolyts, an event that was quite novel and intriguing, because they would turn up on Uncle Doug's motor bike. There was Uncle Doug, pulling off his old fashioned goggles to reveal a grimy, smiling face. There was Brenda, the plump pillion passenger dismounting awkwardly from the back, and there were our cousins, Robert and Paul, a year younger than me, squatting in the sidecar. How exotic and how wonderful, that they had revved and roared all the way from distant London on a motorbike to our country village!

Most often, however, we would travel to Beckenham in South London, where they lived with Nanny. This was another tortuous experience for my father, for two reasons. First, he hated the driving. And second, he felt uncomfortable during these visits staying with Brenda and her family.

For these journeys, my sister, brother and I would be crammed uncomfortably once again into the back of the green van, our first family car. The route was not as long as the drive to Norfolk, where we went on holiday, but it was more exacting for my fraught father, on account of his dread of negotiating his way through London's hostile streets and dealing with the dense traffic. Each time there was palpable tension in the claustrophobic air of the small van. It didn't help that the van was prone to overheating and breaking down.

At first, the trip would be relatively pleasant, as the van rattled its way down the tree and hedgerow-lined A1 to London. But then, as we reached the conurbation and turned down Mill Hill, the traffic would immediately become threatening and unpredictable. There were two or even three lanes of cars and lorries jostling for position on such narrow roads. Tall buildings either side towered over the streets, making them so oppressive and disquieting. There was hardly air to breathe!

The Edgeware Road was straightforward. Direct to Marble Arch with no deviation. The one-way systems after that were designed to confuse country folk, however. Cars hurtled in all directions. There was no conversation in the van. We had learnt to be quiet. Mum just looked around wide-eyed. Dad, sweating by now, was cursing softly under his breath and gripping the steering wheel as it his life depended on it.

Somehow, we found our way to the Embankment. Look – the river Thames – how grand! How majestic! How muddy! The Blackwall Tunnel meant we were making progress. It would take us under the river to south London. Another half an hour, if we didn't take a wrong turn. Finally, to Beckenham and the large gloomy house in which Brenda lived. A huge sigh of relief from Dad as we pulled up, and a joyous smile from Mum, whose face lit up at the prospect of being with her beloved sister and mother. For the children, just relief we had made it without too many arguments or parental nervous breakdowns; and curious anticipation at playing with our cousins and exploring this unfamiliar environment of bricks, smoky smells and traffic din.

Dad wasn't himself during the stay. He didn't say much and seemed quieter than usual. I'm sure he had a good time with Uncle Doug down the pub, when they went off together to leave the women chatting, endlessly reminiscing, laughing a lot like schoolgirls, and drinking cup after cup of tea.

Mum said that Nanny thought Dad too serious when they met and it took them a long time to "warm up". Maybe they didn't warm up enough. Anyway Dad always preferred being at home and didn't like staying with other people. For him, St Ippolyts was the best place in the world. He knew this because he had been to Europe in the war.

I liked these visits, because the place was so different from home and it was interesting to see London. Also Brenda and Doug were kind and amusing and we played happily with our cousins. Brenda was not as good looking as my mother, but she was more confident and outgoing. Cheerful, fussy and maternal, she smothered her children and nephews and nieces with affection, to the extent I felt suffocated sometimes. She was unselfconsciously plump and busied herself cooking, cleaning, gossiping and tending to her brood. She was happy with this role in life, which revolved around her adored children and husband.

Handsomely round-faced, with a generous shock of slicked-back wavy brown hair, Uncle Doug sauntered through life with a smile and a twinkle in his eye. I see him, standing in the kitchen, wielding frying pan and spatula, preparing monumental fried breakfasts. His rotund belly is covered only with a sleeveless vest and the braces which hold up his baggy trousers. From his mouth dangles a cigarette. The smell of hot lard mingled with tobacco stimulates the senses and excites the appetite.

Uncle Doug orders us children around like a comic sergeant major. "Alright, you 'orrible lot, get yer bums over 'ere and sit down quick. No slacking. Otherwise you'll miss yer breakfast!"

I understood from family gossip that Uncle Doug wasn't very successful in his career. He had been an insurance salesman like Dad, but didn't like it. Unlike Dad he was talented at practical things, such as painting and decorating, and made extra money through part-time work. He always had relaxed attitude and enjoyed life. He relished a pint at the pub and a regular flutter on the horses.

He would sit behind the back door, still in his vest, smoking his pipe, and admiring the garden he so skilfully and tenderly cultivated.

"Look at that," he would say, "That's beautiful, just beautiful." Dad said he wasn't very ambitious, but I don't think Doug cared about material ambition.

It was a strange house where they lived. I couldn't understand that it wasn't their house. It seems strangers lived in the upstairs part of this spacious, high-ceilinged, draughty place where footsteps and whispers echoed and lingered in the hallways and corners. We all lived in the tiny back room, which led out to the garden through French windows. This was invariably overheated with a coal fire and smelt of cooked food. We youngsters slept, however, on sofas in the front room, which was spooky. It had poor lighting, which cast shadows into the corners and high ceilings on which images from the street danced menacingly at night. Street lamps, car headlights, alien and unfamiliar glimpses of the city, glimmered in the shadows. The room had a heavy odour of damp and woollen blankets. A wide hall led from the front door, which was never used, direct to a broad staircase leading up into the darkness of the first floor. Strangers lived up there, but I never saw them. I was never even sure where the adults slept. This was Nanny's house, but she let Brenda and Doug live there. However, it wasn't her house, but somebody else's. All very confusing.

The whole situation was quite abnormal, as London itself was abnormal. Coming from a quiet village in the country, we found the capital intimidating. It was an assault on the senses. Too many people rushing around. Too much traffic, which meant you could hardly cross the road. London even smelt unpleasantly of petrol fumes and asphalt, floor polish and fried food. Too much noise surrounded you, even at night when you tried to sleep.

Where were the birds and the sound of owls at night? Where was the cawing of crows in the day time? Our poor cousins, I thought, had no recreation ground at the end of their garden, as we did. They had no allotments or fields to run in, or play armies, or trees to climb on. They were trapped in the small yard at the back, with its high brick walls enclosing them. I was always so glad I lived in the village. There was space to breathe and time to daydream.

Nevertheless, we got on well with our cousins. Sister Sue, younger brother Geoff and I spent many contented hours with Robert and Paul, our twin cousins, who were one year younger than me. They had a younger sister, Elizabeth, much fawned over by everyone, but, as still an infant, she didn't warrant too much attention from me.

The twins were like chalk and cheese, though very close to each other and supportive. Paul was more like his father, quick-witted, amusing and sometimes sarcastic. Round-faced and alert, he was clever and showed a prodigal interest in engines and matters mechanical. He wasn't particularly athletic or good at sports, but interested enough to make him worthwhile company.

Whereas Paul was fair haired, Robert was black-haired and unlike his twin in most respects. He was gentler and not so clever, but more sympathetic than his brother – more affectionate and lacking any malice whatsoever. Despite their differences the boys got along well, constantly teasing each other, but without serious intent. Robert did share Paul's interest in motors, however, and that was common ground which had little appeal to me.

Nevertheless, we would all pass the time together harmoniously in the narrow garden, with its unfriendly fortress walls, on the mud patch which passed for a lawn. We would fashion out ball games, chasing games and French cricket, which didn't need much room. There were toy bows and arrows with rubber suckers to shoot and a kind of hand tennis. Whatever we played it was inevitably competitive for us boys, particularly between myself and Paul. Robert was too sweet-natured to worry about the results of the games and my sister wasn't interested.

This childish one-upmanship mirrored our mothers' constant rivalry. Those two, as twins, regularly compared and commented on the achievements of their offspring. Whilst this was never bitter, it was ongoing and wearying. We were made aware of it. Did I know, my mother would ask, that Paul had come top of the class in maths? This was put to me, not so much as to motivate me, but make sure it was my responsibility to make sure that my mother wasn't embarrassed by this in the future. "Did we know that Paul had passed his 25-yard swimming certificate?" I didn't take this suggestiveness too seriously as I was clearly superior in the most important skill – playing football. That's what mattered to me.

These visits were quite tolerable. It was always good to see Nanny, who was kind and had had a terrible life, we were constantly reminded. The house itself was weird – not like a proper home – and had strange odours, but it was fascinating in its way, slightly bizarre. Mum had a wonderful time, gossiping and giggling with Brenda, talking family trivia and memories nonstop. But the few days, and that's all we ever stayed, passed by quickly. We were soon on the way back, rattling through the grey streets of London, before emerging onto the A1.

It was a relief to get home, where there were normal sounds and smells. Our village was so calm, green and spacious. We could run again in the recreation ground or across the fields. We could walk in the lanes without worrying about never-ending streams of traffic. I was always thankful that I lived here, in a village, and not in London, which was so colourless and claustrophobic in comparison.

Chapter Eleven
Secret Preacher

Between 1658 and 1661, as Oliver Cromwell's Commonwealth crumbled before the forces of the monarchist restoration, there were strange, secretive happenings on the outskirts of the village of St Ippolyts. On frequent occasions, on dark nights, hundreds of folk from the parish, the neighbouring town of Hitchin, and from surrounding villages, would creep furtively into the woods lying to the west of the parish for illegal gatherings.

They had to be stealthy and vigilant. Watchmen would be set to look out for any sign of the magistrates or their cronies. For these meetings were beyond the pale. They were coming together to hear the inspiring oratory of an exceptional but unlawful preacher, who rose from obscurity to become one of the most famous Christian authors in the English language. This preacher was John Bunyan, later renowned worldwide for his morality tale "Pilgrim's Progress".

The undercover worshippers were heading for Wain Wood, a picturesque and suitably secluded spot where they might listen to Bunyan undisturbed. Named after a "wain" or "wagon track", the wood was covered in oak, hornbeam and larch, with a bed of flowers in the spring. It was a valuable source of firewood for the locals. More importantly, it was thick enough to provide cover for Bunyan's clandestine sermons.

Considered a deviant radical by the conservative Church of England, the preacher Bunyan found fertile ground for his ideas in the North Hertfordshire area. Not only had he family ties – his aunt lived in Hitchin – but the town had shown early leanings towards the various nonconformist movements springing up during the Commonwealth.

Before Cromwell's ascendancy to the Protectorate, as he called it, the Hitchin dissenters would have been forced underground by Archbishop Laud's high church administration. After the execution of Laud and his master, Charles 1, however, the debate was in the open and the different sects prospered. Among them, the Baptists gained popularity, but did not, we read, enjoy a "gathered church."

Within this climate of heated religious debate John Bunyan flourished like an exotic plant. In 1658, he was chosen by the leader of the Baptist church in Bedford – Pastor Gifford – to spread the good word to the surrounding parishes. Hitchin, and St Ippolyts, became regular stops on his evangelical circuit.

He hadn't always been such a saintly character, though. Born in a village near Bedford in 1628, his father was a tinker – a mender of pots and pans. Young John, who was notorious for being particularly foul-mouthed, picked up some book-reading as well as metal working skills, before being pressed into the Parliamentary Army at the tender age of sixteen. Between 1644 and 1647, he trailed around with the Roundhead army, probably passing through Hitchin. The town's militias certainly fought with the Parliamentarians.

Nevertheless, it was in the ranks that he fell under the spell of the radical preachers, among them the Baptists, with their belief in adult, full-immersion baptism, salvation through good works and rejection of the Church of England's priestly hierarchy. On leaving the military life he nurtured his innate talent for sermonising and pamphleteering, producing over sixty expansive sermons, until he caught the eye of Pastor Gifford.

However, it was not for his pamphlets or his preaching in St Ippolyts that made him a figure of universal standing in the Christian realm, but his subsequent imprisonment. His twelve years' incarceration in Bedford gaol were spent producing Pilgrim's Progress, a tale of Christian endeavour, temptation and reward, that was a best-seller of his day and turned him into a celebrity.

His tribulations began immediately after the Restoration of the monarchy in 1660. The new regime cracked down on the sects and any deviation from the Church of England orthodoxy was harshly dealt with. In 1664, the so-called Conventicle Act outlawed unofficial gatherings of more than four persons for worship. A first offence would mean jail for three months or a fine of five pounds. But a third offence would result in transportation for seven years!

Bunyan was arrested in 1661 and thrown into prison by magistrate Francis Wingate; "...for devilishly and perniciously abstaining from coming to church and for being a common upholder of unlawful meetings and conventicles to the great disturbance and distraction of the good subjects of this kingdom."

Sarcastically, the magistrate further condemned Bunyan because he "presumed to mend souls as well as kettles and pots."

At first his sentence was three months, but Bunyan violated the terms by stubbornly resuming preaching immediately upon release, for which offence the term was extended to a punishing twelve years.

On release, however, he finally completed his master work. By 1677, he had moved to London and the book was published the following year – to general acclaim. Bunyan continued his preaching and proselytising until his death in 1688. This occurred, ironically, the year before the Glorious Revolution, and the return to tolerance which allowed nonconformists, like the Baptists, to worship in public without fear of retribution. In 1692, the first Baptist Church was built in Hitchin.

Bunyan left a lasting impression on the district and on the village of St Ippolyts. His subversive services attracted up to 1000 worshippers at a time, all trooping devoutly to Wain Wood in the darkness. There in a hollow, resembling a natural amphitheatre, Bunyan would hold his admiring congregation spellbound. He would often be disguised as a farmer, with pitch fork as a prop, to smuggle him there undetected. Even the weather would not deter them and when it rained four devoted ladies would hold a tarpaulin over his head as he castigated the established Church and extolled the principles of the Baptist belief.

His legacy can still be detected in that quiet spot, forever known as Bunyan's Dell; but more profoundly in the spirit of independent thinking, self-responsibility and distrust of blind authority, that infused Christian thinking in the years following his passing. St Ippolyts rightly claims a small stake in the progress of the remarkable pilgrim that was John Bunyan.

Chapter Twelve
Inkwells and Jesus

Learning was all-important, for education meant a route to a better life. It offered the chance to become a solicitor, a doctor or an accountant, and the opportunity to earn good money. This we were taught by Mum and Dad, neither of whom had enjoyed much schooling. My mother, on losing her father at the age of eight, had been shipped off with her twin sister to a dismal charitable school for female orphans. There she spent eminently forgettable years wearing scratchy thick blue woollen stockings all year round and long gym slips until the age of fifteen. Apart from being goalkeeper to the second eleven at hockey, which filled her with dread, and put her off sport for life, she had few stories or memories of school to tell us. That's testimony enough as to the unimaginative greyness of the institution.

What a waste! My mother was an intelligent and sensitive person who would have blossomed in the right educational context. But she had lost all interest in books and conjecture. Her curiosity had been dulled. She was preoccupied with domesticity and family security. That was enough. However, she still recognised the value of learning and encouraged us children, in a gentle way, with our learning, without getting obsessive about it.

My father was more ambitious for us. He too, had left school early, at fourteen, as was normal for those of his status and generation. A career in the Co-op may have been his fate had it not been for the Second World War. Conscription plucked him from his bicycle-riding deliveries and fortunately, he stayed safe and unharmed, away from frontline action. He also found out that he was relatively intelligent and learnt a trade – communications – rising to sergeant in the ranks. He wanted us to benefit from the new educational opportunities that post-war Britain offered. Education was necessary to gain social status and economic well-being.

This process started at the idyllic St Ippolyts Primary School, where my older sister, Sue, me, and my younger brother, Geoff, all took our first steps in learning. It was the same school where my father had been taught, from the age of eight to fourteen. Built just before the great 1848 revolutions in Europe, the main part of the school remained unchanged when I attended. It was a flint and brick construction, sited on top of St Ippolyts hill, immediately opposite the Norman church.

When I started, at four years old, the school had been extended – two, new, red-brick classrooms having been added just after the war. Altogether, the building offered four classrooms, dining room, toilets and staff facilities. In addition, it was the home of the headmaster, Mr Sergeant, a gruff, military type, who was bossy but well-meaning. He always wore a pin-striped suit, like a City gent. The two modern classrooms catered for the four to five-year class of Miss Morris, and the six to seven-year class or Mrs Austin. Then from eight to nine we were taught by the gentle and soft-spoken Mr Livingstone in the old building, before the austere final two years with Mr Sergeant. He drummed into us the critical importance for our entire future lives of passing the Eleven Plus. This was serious and would decide our fate.

Our school sat immediately at the top of the hill, on a quiet lane which led from the main London-Hitchin road, and ran through the upper village. Apart from the church opposite, there were just a few cottages further up the road, but otherwise the building was surrounded by green fields and woods. Behind the school was our tarmac playground, which lay at the bottom of a sloping playing field, some hundred yards long. Here we spent every moment of our break times, winter and summer.

About one hundred pupils attended the school, approximately twenty-five in each of the four classes. Nearly everyone walked to school, from the nearby upper village of St Ippolyts, the lower reaches of the village of Gosmore and the in-between Waterdell Lane community, of which we were a part. A few, coming from outlying farms, were driven in, but most of us had a journey of less than half an hour. For me, sister Sue and brother Geoff, this meant a twenty-minute walk along the curving Waterdell Lane, up to the London Road. Here we would be ushered over by the lollipop lady, come rain or shine. Finally, we had to cover ten minutes up the hill, past the iron foundry and Brook End farm to arrive for our nine o'clock start. Very few adults came with us. It was safe enough and thought quite reasonable that we made our own way there.

Sue, two years older than me, had taken charge of me on the way. When she had left to go on to secondary school in Hitchin, it was left to me to take my younger brother Geoff, who was four years my junior. I resented this greatly, because I didn't want the responsibility of looking after him. I made this quite clear to him, which only added to his misery of being dependent on his inconsiderate older brother.

We all started with Miss Morris. She was young and enthusiastic and wore a pleated woollen skirt and sturdy brown shoes. This was a gentle, if quite formal introduction to the world of education. We sat in rows in a bright, cheerful classroom, adorned with colourful pictures we had drawn, maps and nature diagrams, showing birds, trees and plants. I remember a lot of drawing and learning to write with wax crayons. We began reading with simple primers, learning through phonics, step by step, and practising some simple arithmetic too. She read us stories and took us on nature walks.

Then, from six to eight for class two, we were ushered next door into the capable and efficient hands of Mrs Austin, whom we called "Miss" of course. She was older, matronly and bustling, expecting more from us and pushing us to learn our arithmetic, multiplication tables and reading with more structure and repetition.

This led us into class three with Mr Livingstone. His classroom was in the older part of the school building, gloomy, with a high ceiling and windows that didn't let much light in. It had old fashioned desks, dark brown with bench seats attached, stained with generations of ink stains, scratchings and carvings from pupils long departed. Now the learning process accelerated. There were compositions to write, in joined up writing, multiplication and division to master, even some elementary geography to absorb. Mr Livingstone, with his dishevelled shock of white hair, thin face and body, grey slacks and tweed jacket with leather patches on the elbows, guided us like a benign apparition floating around the room. There were no harsh words, anger or frustration from that dedicated man, only encouragement and humour as he prepared us for the rigours of the world.

I particularly liked this teacher. First and foremost, he took us for football, which meant he rated highly with me, though he was the most unathletic figure, who probably never kicked a ball in his life. Nevertheless, he coached us with enthusiasm and sound knowledge and turned our village team, with barely enough students in the upper classes to form the eleven, into a force to be reckoned with in the North Hertfordshire area. Why, we beat Wilbury and Baldock and Pirton, all bigger schools than us. We even overcame the mighty Wilshere Dacre, largest school in Hitchin. Three of us went on to play for North Herts. Admittedly, we lost one of our two games 11-1 to Barnet, but Mr Livingstone thought they had cheated by playing older boys and Dad was pleased with me because I scored our solitary goal.

But Mr Livingstone also cultivated other talents. He encouraged our creative writing and I was especially praised for my report on the 1959 Cup Final when Luton Town had been tragically defeated by Nottingham Forest. Although it took me some weeks to accept the disappointment I found that my journalistic exercise helped recovery. Mr Livingstone thought it good enough to adorn the classroom wall for some weeks. I resolved then and there that as well as being a professional footballer I would also be a journalist. After all, footballers were limited to a five pound a week maximum wage, so a second income, as Dad pointed out, was needed to ensure a decent holiday once a year.

In addition to this, our benign mentor also encouraged a thespian spirit among his village charges. He had us act in mysterious plays, most of which we didn't understand

and some of which he wrote himself. Memorable amongst these was a tale of the American Revolution. I played Paul Revere, the swashbuckling hero of the rebels. This caused my mother considerable stress as she had to help make my costume. She spent some hours sewing a sash across an old blazer and ruffs onto the sleeves of an old shirt. I wore my cowboy hat, pinned up on one side and with a feather in it, my Dad's leather belt, into which I stuffed a plastic sword and toy pistol, and Tony Wyman's cowboy boots. In this outlandish costume I appeared in the play performed at Mr Livingstone's bungalow. A baffled and amused, but polite audience of adoring parents supported us throughout and applauded proudly. I remembered almost all the words and needed few prompts.

As much as Mr Livingstone had coaxed our creativity from us, equally so did the military Mr Sergeant drill educational discipline and precision into us when we graduated to his class four. No messing about now. This was preparing us for the test of our lives. The selection process that would determine our future. Either we would make it to Hitchin Boys' Grammar School, from whence we would likely go to university or at least a professional role, or we would be packed off to the Bessemer Secondary Modern, which we would probably leave at fifteen to enter a factory, apprenticeship or, if we were lucky, a junior administrative position. Such were the binary outcomes of the Eleven Plus.

Mr Sergeant would make sure that none of us would fail through lack of effort. A considerate but booming man, who overawed us with his presence and volume, he made us recite, read, repeat and revise constantly. Now there were no football essays or plays, but grammar exercises and writing practice, endless writing practice. There were long divisions, fractions, decimals and multiple multiplications.

We sat, in regimented rows, in that gloomy classroom, where the windows were too high to look out of, at desks scored with the scratchings of generations of village students. There was discipline, but I don't remember him ever caning anyone, not even the naughtiest among us. There was no need, for the cane was ever present, in his hand or on his desk, like the sword of Damocles, its threat sufficient to inspire diligent obedience. We all understood, it was for our own good and Mr Sergeant was there to help us.

The greatest torment of this time was writing. Left-handers like myself (at least we were no longer forced to change or punished for our perverse habit) had to overcome the challenge of ink and nib pens. Although the age of ball-point pens was upon us, a merciful invention, we had to learn to write fluent copperplate with these instruments of torture instead. How was a left hander to avoid his following palm, in writing from left to right, from smudging the very words he was supposed to be faultlessly crafting?

I tried stretching my holding hand above the writing line and by curling my fingers back to point the pen towards me I might avoid touching the paper. But this just induced cramps in the wrist. Then I tried keeping my hand below the writing line and pointing the pen upwards. This was less painful and avoiding smudging, but resulted in backward leaning letters, and Mr Sergeant didn't approve of backward leaning script.

The compromise was a stiff upright style that might lead a psychologist to conclude I was unimaginative, conventional and formulaic. But none of this was true. It was just a coping strategy, to deal with the world of inkwells and ink. It was everywhere. Ink monitors filled inkwells, which sat in small holes in the desk. Ancient ink stained deep in the grain of the wooden desks. Contemporary ink caused drops, ink blots, ink smudges. Ink seeped onto the fingers, and even on the white school shirts. There was no escaping until the education system finally agreed to accept the modern technology of ballpoint pens, which had been around for years.

As well as writing and arithmetic we learnt some elementary geography and history. This reinforced our deep self-confidence in the superiority of British culture. Was not the large globe that Mr Sergeant spun occasionally and jabbed at, largely red to indicate the British Empire and Commonwealth? MacMillan's *Wind of Change* had hardly rustled any leaves in Africa. Despicable terrorists in Malaysia, Kenya and Aden were fighting for independence when it was clear their peoples were better off under the just and democratic British colonial rule, symbolised by the Union Jack and the Queen herself. India was independent, but, as Winston Churchill said, and my father repeated in agreement, perhaps that step had been a mistake. Winston Churchill, though no longer in power, still strode across the political landscape like a colossus, his grandiloquent wartime exhortations echoing in the nation's consciousness.

We had still celebrated Empire Day up to Mr Livingstone's class and now we marked Commonwealth Day. Both were to remind us how the United Kingdom had civilised half the world. The monarchy was revered and there was great excitement on one occasion when we were told that the Queen would drive through St Ippolyts – our village – on her way somewhere.

People in the village were already quite proud of our royal connections, for the Queen Mother herself, from the aristocratic Bowes-Lyon family, had spent time in Hatfield and Knebworth House, which was barely a few miles away!

But the Queen's "visit" was special. We were warned to wear our very best and checked for clean faces and hands, before being marched in platoons down St Ippolyts Hill, and past the foundry, to the main London Road. Here we were lined up in orderly fashion and joined by a number of enthusiastic parents, though mine didn't show any interest at all. We were each given a small paper union jack on a stick and red-and-white bunting to hold. And so we waited, and waited, in the warm sunshine, feeling increasingly uncomfortable. I hated standing still like that.

Finally, a shiver of excitement, as the instruction came. "Get ready to wave your flags, she's coming!" We craned forward on the pavement, looking down the road for the carriage, for it surely would be a horse-drawn carriage, wouldn't it? No, gilded carriages were replaced by black limousines – three of them. They glided past, slowing down momentarily to allow the village yokels a glimpse of royalty. It was impossible to see anything. I didn't see the Queen, giving her famous stiff wave. I wasn't even sure which car she was in. None of us were. We waved and cheered her on her way, before the sombre cavalcade disappeared down the road towards Hitchin, our shrill voices petered out and a disappointed silence fell on us all.

I wondered why she couldn't have stopped for a few minutes to talk to us, as she was often seen chatting to crowds on the television. Couldn't she have wound down the window and waved to us so we could see her face? Our teachers were as disappointed as us, but explained that she had important functions to attend and had to make sure she wasn't late. And we were only a small village after all. The bunting and flags were collected ready for the next royal visit and we trudged back up the hill in twos to our dingy classroom. When I told Dad later he only said, "What would you expect, they're royalty?"

Life at school was not all taken up with work, even in Mr Sergeant's class. Generally, the boys and girls in that cohort socialised well together, with few fights or disagreements.

We all ate together in the small hall, including the teachers, who supervised us. Mothers acted as dinner ladies, providing us with a wholesome and nutritious, if entirely unimaginative fare. Meat, greens and potatoes was the standard combination, with pudding made of pies and tarts with thick custard. This offered no particular challenge to any of us, though we did offer futile rebellion sometimes against the convention that everything had to be eaten.

My own special hate was sago pudding, a cheap dessert course regularly supplied. I wasn't the taste so much as the consistency, which reminded me of frog spawn. I simply couldn't swallow it and the teachers' admonition that I couldn't leave the table until it was devoured turned a problem of the gullet into a psychological drama. I circumvented it at first by inducing retching and running off to the boys' toilet. When that dramatic ploy became too obvious I would simply slip my portion onto someone else's plate, who didn't share my aversion to the slippery pudding and was greedy enough to eat everything on offer.

Every day, unless there was rain, we spent our playtimes, morning, lunchtime and afternoon, on the play area at the back of the school. We had an asphalt playground, about the size of a basketball court, set level at the bottom of a sloping grassy field. Normally, the boys played soccer with a small plastic ball, or hand tennis, or paddle, a game where you had to hit your quarry with a thrown ball. The quarry ran between two opposing lines trying to avoid the usually painful contact. Meanwhile the girls played at skipping, two of them holding the rope, while the third danced in and out of the swinging rope, while they chanted traditional rhymes and songs. At other times they played varieties of hopscotch, hitching up their gymslips into their pants.

There were the seasonal games too, like conkers in the autumn. Several weeks of intense competition, searching for that elusive "sixer", followed. Various underhand ploys took place, to ensure that your conker was harder than your opponents'. You could soak it in vinegar, or bake it in the oven, but, ultimately the accuracy of your strike was more important, as your weapon was swung at the end of its six-inch string to smash your opponent's weapon.

In winter, when the playground was covered in ice and snow, we were sent outside as normal, whatever the temperature. Fresh air was healthy. On the playground us boys would create lengthy slides on the asphalt surface, seeing who the glide the furthest. But after a broken arm one winter and other injuries, Mr Sergeant would come and put salt on our exciting ice game and scold us. We waited until he had gone and then started another one.

At intervals the whole class would be led down the hill to the village hall, which lay just across the London Road. Here we would learn country dancing, which I found excruciatingly embarrassing. First, it didn't seem to me, or my father, a real pastime for a boy. Second, we had to choose a partner and dance with her. I didn't mind picking on Patsy Sawyer, who was probably the cleverest girl in the class and quite pretty, but I knew this would result in some embarrassing teasing from my parents and my older sister, who would assert that Patsy was my girlfriend. Although I liked girls I had no need for a girlfriend and the idea of kissing was definitely not for a boy.

The only occasion when kissing did appear to be acceptable was at birthday parties. One game we often played was Postman's Knock, which required one of the party to go outside the room, knock on the door and state who they would like to kiss. The lucky partner would go outside, kiss the caller and then remain outside for their turn. This proved quite enjoyable as it was a group activity, unless of course you were never chosen, in which case the whole game was just miserable.

Another problem with kissing and getting involved with girls was that these habits were frowned upon by adults, an attitude reinforced by the church and the vicar, who obviously knew right from wrong. As we were a Church of England School, we often saw our vicar, who came frequently to talk to us about Jesus, the Ten Commandments and generally how to be a good person.

Up to the time of moving into Mr Sergeant's top class I had been a sporadic attendee at Sunday School, but subsequently given up the practice. I had neither disliked it nor enjoyed the experience, my overriding impression being that it was a cold and bleak way of spending a Sunday morning. My sister and I were sent along at a young age, because that was what was expected of village children.

I remembered sitting uncomfortably on small wooden stools in the village church. It was an impressive enough structure, which went back to ancient times, but I found it austere and unfriendly, with its bare stone walls and flagstone floors contrasting unfavourably with the carpeted security of home.

So we would sit, listening while the vicar told us tales of Jesus, the Son of God, or his assistants would read to us from picture books about parables and miracles. We would listen out of politeness and curiosity, because the stories were fascinating, if cruel at times, and thus we absorbed the teaching of the mother church, which would be imprinted on our minds forever. Distant, but always smiling, the vicar spoke in a funny voice, especially when he read from the bible, like he was moaning in pain – but I assumed it was to sound holy.

We would also colour in picture books with fat wax crayons, lying on rush mats on the cold stone, or draw our own pictures of Jesus' travails. Palm Sunday – Jesus riding on a donkey while people threw palms before him; the trial with Pontius Pilate; the brutal Romans beating him and making him wear a crown of thorns; and finally crucifying him. He was clearly a very good and brave man, but I couldn't quite understand why he had to die in this way and how did it mean that he saved us from our sins?

Other stories were easier to grasp. For example, the Good Samaritan showed how you should help people in trouble. Jesus was kind to poor people, children and crippled people and washed their feet sometimes. Yes, he demonstrated how to be a better person, but I wasn't sure about turning the other cheek all the time. Didn't you have to fight back sometimes against evil, like we did against the Nazis and Japs? I also had my doubts about the miracles. Did he really turn water into wine, and feed five thousand people with two fish and five loaves. It sounded far-fetched.

Dad thought that Jesus was a special person who was an example to the people of his time, but it was exaggerated to say he was the son of god. He said Christianity taught people how to live in a civilised way and gave us rules for living by. I thought Dad's explanation was better than the vicar's. Jesus was inspiring though and I could understand how some adventurous types became missionaries to convert savage tribes in Africa. I could see myself as Dr Livingstone, explorer and missionary, but I would always take a Tommy gun with me in case of attack.

Whilst I agreed with the Church about the way of living and code of conduct, I never really warmed to the rituals. However, when the church organ and choir were in full voice, or when we all sang hymns like *Onward Christian Soldiers* together I felt uplifted, but I experienced awkwardness when it came to prayers and chants and sermons and services. By the time I was ten I had stopped going to Sunday School. I reckoned I was a good person anyway and that God would see this.

Preferring action to spirituality I decided instead to join the cub scouts. Here was an environment where the code of ethics was more military. Baden-Powell's patriotic call to training, outdoor pursuits and self-reliance was interpreted for the under 11s. Afterwards we might graduate into becoming Boy Scouts, and then perhaps Cadets, or Territorials, or even regular soldiers (as National Service had just ended), accepting the call to duty, to defend the Commonwealth against subversive revolutionaries.

Our uniform was green (camouflage?). We wore grey socks with green top hoops, grey or khaki shorts, a brown shirt, a green sweater, onto which badges of distinction could be sewn by impatient mothers, a cap and a neckerchief, fastened by a toggle. A toggle was a small leather ring though which the two ends of the neckerchief passed. Much easier than knotting a tie!

Suitably attired we would, before each weekly session in the village hall, or, in summer, just outside it, stand in a circle and recite our paean to duty. "We will DOB, DOB, DOB", we chanted robotically, assuring Akela, our adult leader, that we would, indeed Do Our Best in response to his "DYB, DYB, DYB" (Do Your Best) command.

Then on to the real part, learning activities – map reading, marches, fire-lighting, use of penknives, games. Inside the village hall, on the cold nights – we always met on a Monday evening – paddle, British Bulldog and tag. We also learned useful things like different knots and how to tell birds apart. I enjoyed it. In the summer, it was even better. We learnt how to pitch tents and went on small hikes into the countryside, learning about landmarks, and trees and the lie of the land. All very vital if the Soviets ever invaded our village.

Also in the summer came "Bob-a-Job" week. This was an exercise in junior enterprise, designed to raise funds for the troop, while benefiting a grateful community. We were unleashed upon the parish, in pairs, each covering a specific set of roads and houses. Knocking boldly on doors, we offered our services for any kind of chore, in return for a "bob" or old shilling.

The response to this generous offer of free labour was greeted in various ways. A few happily gave us the money just to go away. The majority, momentarily puzzled but interested in getting their money's worth, gave us reasonable tasks, such as weeding the front path, sweeping the back yard, or washing the car. A few were exploitative. One man had us dig over the whole of his back garden vegetable patch, which had been neglected. It took two of us the entire afternoon, but our reward was no more than the regulation shilling. He didn't even offer us a drink. This exercise was quite competitive, with each pairing aiming to collect more than the others. Our Akela encouraged this competition.

This was not surprising, for Mr Skeggs, our Akela, or troop leader, was himself a businessman, being the owner of the iron foundry, our village's only industrial enterprise. He was dutiful and gave his time voluntarily, but I found him lacking in humour.

My doubts were exacerbated one Christmas, when his lack of character became all too apparent to me. I had decided that we, the troop, should buy our Akela a Christmas gift. This would prove to him my generosity, leadership and no doubt ingratiate myself with him. Consequently, I rallied my fellow wolf cubs, and persuaded them to cough up coins from their limited pocket money. In the end I was able to gather the princely sum of three shillings and sixpence. Enriched with this contribution I headed off to Woolworths in Hitchin, which is where I bought all my Christmas presents. Having selected what I thought was the perfect gift for an Akela – a Swiss army style penknife which even included an implement for taking stones out of a horse's hoof – I wrapped it ready for presentation.

This moment turned out to be a major disappointment. At the last meeting before the Christmas break I presented the gift to him on behalf of the others. Akela tore open the brown paper wrapping, looked at the knife, said thank you, put it in his pocket and just carried on with the meeting. I had at least expected special recognition for my initiative and careful selection of gift. But this didn't materialise and no more was said of the matter. Perhaps he had a lot of knives already, I reasoned, but I never forgave him for not showering me with praise.

It was only a few months later that I left the Wolf Cubs. Matters came to a head over the shoe-cleaning badge. I had already collected four of five badges, for proving myself skilful in certain tasks, like erecting a tent and lighting a fire, so cleaning shoes was simple. I spent a good half an hour in the village hall one evening, polishing and shining a pair of black shoes I had been given, and they literally shone like mirrors when I had finished. However, when Akela inspected them he informed me that I had not passed the test satisfactorily. His reason was that I had made too much mess, including the fact that both my arms were black with shoe polish half way up to the elbows.

I failed to see what that had to do with cleaning the shoes so brilliantly, and my trust in Akela was broken. That night I decided the injustice was simply too great and that I would not return again the pack. I never did go back and I never became a Boy Scout.

In another way I was relieved. Going all the way to the village hall on a Monday night, particularly in winter, was challenging. It was at least a mile distant and I had to go all the way along Waterdell Lane, in the dark, on my own, at least up to Francis Porter's house, where Francis often joined me.

The return home, at nine o'clock at night, drew on all my reserves of courage. The nights were pitch black and barely illuminated by the infrequent and dingy street lights. I countered this by running all the way, so no evil doers could catch me, and fortifying myself by whistling loudly. Even then the unexpected call of an owl would set my heart racing. I was pleased to avoid this ordeal.

Meanwhile, my primary school days were drawing to an end and the greatest challenge in my life so far loomed – the Eleven Plus exam. It was made very clear to us at school that this would make or break us. Mr Sergeant had earmarked a few of us as probables while the rest weren't given too much attention. We were coached and cajoled, given practice papers and routines. It was all about Arithmetic and English.

My older sister Sue had already paved the way, having passed the exam two years previously and progressed well at the Girl's Grammar School. In so doing she had become the first Wingate ever to reach these lofty academic levels. I was expected to follow her example. However, I did not feel too pressured. After all, many of my friends, Martin, Colin, Jamie and Graham, assumed they were going to the Bessemer School, so even if I failed, I would be in good company.

Furthermore, another factor had to be considered. At the Boys' Grammar School they only played Rugby and Hockey, but no football. The ex-public school headmaster of the Boys' Grammar had replaced football with rugby only a few years before, in order to raise the social status of the place. I was well aware that going to the grammar school may well hinder my ambition to become a professional footballer.

When the big day finally arrived and we sat looking at the overturned exam papers on our desks and waited for Mr Sergeant to say "You may begin", I didn't feel particularly nervous, rather fatalistic. There followed several hours of scratching around with our awful nib pens, trying as ever to avoid blots and smudges. I found the English questions easy enough, and struggled with one or two of the arithmetic problems. When it was over, I was ready to get out onto the playground to run around and cast back hardly a thought. Whatever the outcome, I would be fine.

However, I was jolted from my post-exam reverie by Mr Sergeant, who summoned me from the playground into his classroom. I was naturally concerned that I had made some major blunder, but he pulled me to his side at his desk and opened my arithmetic paper.

"Look here," he said, "Look at this one again. What do think is the right answer?" I recognised immediately I had made a mistake. "Well, as you know the right answer, just change it here," he told me, pointing out the exact spot on the exam paper. So I did. I altered the answer. "Good," he concluded. "That's better, now you can go out and play again."

I didn't find anything wrong with this incident, for if Mr Sergeant was in charge of the exam it must be part of the normal procedure. After all, he was our Headmaster. Furthermore, I really did know the right answer, once he had shown me.

A few weeks later I found out that I had passed the Eleven Plus. Only two boys and two girls out of our class of twenty-five made it through. I would be heading for the Boys' Grammar School. I was pleased that my parents and teachers were satisfied, though the idea of going to the grammar school was not without doubts. I would, after all, have to mix with the boys from the town, with posh boys and with very intelligent boys, while I was just a village boy.

Nevertheless, I had been well prepared. Grounded in arithmetic and writing, my academic foundations were solid. My moral compass had been set by the Church of England and my loyalty to Queen and country embedded. I was ready for the wider world. I regretted that the grammar school didn't play football, but at least I would be allowed to use a proper fountain pen or at least a ballpoint.

Chapter Thirteen
Education. Education. Education.

In 1843, the village of St Ippolyts welcomed a new vicar. He was the Reverend Thomas Henry Steel, who was to live in the parish for over eight years. His legacy was to prove significant and long-lasting, for as well as administering to his flock in the church and saving souls, he was instrumental in establishing formal education by promoting the foundation of the first village school.

Dismayed at the almost universal illiteracy among the sturdy villagers and encouraged by the prevailing church orthodoxy to improve general education, he was prompted to act. Convincing the local Lord of Maydencroft Manor to donate a parcel of land immediately opposite the church, he set about collecting the necessary funds. Through various money-raising schemes and solicitation of grants, the vicar eventually accumulated the required princely sum of £412.90p for the building itself.

Having put the works out to tender, the planners chose a local contractor, Mr Joseph Bates of Stevenage, to erect the new school. By Christmas, 1846, the simple, one school-room structure was complete. Built of brick and local flint, it included rudimentary quarters for the school teacher as well. In March 1847, the first, no doubt slightly bewildered, village students were enrolled.

This local initiative was hardly unique. Nationwide, Church of England schools were springing up, partly as a result of the industrial revolution and partly because of the Church's wish to have an influence over education in a time of intellectual and scientific challenge to the established religious dogmas.

In a rural community such as St Ippolyts, where everyone, apart from the handful of landowners, were farm labourers, there had been no obvious need for learning. For the wealthy, where it was appreciated, learning was conducted at home, with private governesses taking on the role of teachers. Like Charlotte Bronte's Jane Eyre they became a fixture in the house and undertook the tutoring of the young generation.

For the mass of the labouring poor, however, the only limited glimpse of formal education would have been offered through the prism of Sunday school. In the cold corners of the village church, youngsters could once a week get elementary lessons in reading and writing, as well as moralistic tales, using the bible as a text book. As this was restricted in time, and voluntary, the benefits were limited.

In addition, there were plaiting schools, where youngsters, particularly girls, would learn the craft of straw plaiting. For the impoverished labouring families, this provided some additional subsistence income. The plaited strands would be sold at the market in Hitchin, mainly for use in the Luton hat industry. But these "schools" would slowly die out as the state became involved in general education in the second half of the 19th century and as the local plaiting industry collapsed in face of cheap imports.

That first cohort of budding village scholars, who showed up in March 1847, would have been a motley bunch. We can suspect they were unusually well scrubbed and booted, but coming from relative degrees of poverty, presented a serious pedagogical challenge to the young mistress who confronted them that morning.

There were, at first, 43 of them to house in the one same classroom which was, for most of the year, cold and damp. In addition, their ages ranged from three to twelve. They were completely unused to sitting still or studying and the concept of a regular timed day alien to them or their families. Children of non-conformist homes, as well as Church of England, were welcome. Now this was real comprehensive schooling!

Miss Jefford, the young lady hired to overcome this daunting educational challenge, had been hired through the Ecclesiastical Gazette and was certainly well qualified and of unblemished character. She was to be paid a monthly salary of two pounds one shilling and eight pence, plus she could keep one half of the pupils' fees they were required to pay. In addition, she had a local teaching assistant, paid sixpence a week, and another part timer, Miss Ross, who taught plaiting.

Term times would, for some years, be quite fluid, as they had to fit around ploughing and harvest times, and they depended on the weather. Even the younger children would be needed to lend a hand at critical harvest time and the school had to accommodate economic necessity.

Long and demanding for students and teachers alike, the school day began at nine a.m. Lessons proceeded until twelve noon, when pupils went home for lunch. Resuming at two p.m. the afternoon session then went on to ten minutes past four in the Summer. Days would be occupied with lessons in the Holy Scripture and the Catechism, in the three Rs, in geography, singing, and – for the girls' – needlework.

We see from the school logs, kept by the head teachers, that the three Rs were tolerated, but geography provided little interest for the pupils. Their day-to-day horizons would barely stretch to the local market town, never mind the rest of the country or the world beyond! Singing, however, was understandably much appreciated.

For the teachers, attempting to instil some learning into this rainbow collection of village imps, the strains became apparent. Alas, poor Miss Jefford only lasted a few months. Not really surprising, given that student numbers had by May 1847 risen to a nerve-jingling 60! Class discipline must have been an illusory objective. By November of that year Miss Jefford had packed her bags and left, probably exhausted and quite likely a nervous wreck.

In the coming years it remained a perennial problem to retain teachers for the idyllically placed school, but despite this, gradual development was achieved. By 1853, it was recorded that 58% of the village children attended – not bad by national standards.

The difficulty in maintaining attendance, which was not compulsory until 1880, arose from the realities of family economics. In an agricultural community like St Ippolyts, the children were part of the workforce. Even if not allowed to be formally employed after a series of Parliamentary Acts forbidding child labour, they nevertheless had important roles to play. That might have been tending livestock, collecting firewood, gathering acorns for the pigs, or "gleaning," that is, cleaning up the left over grains in the fields after harvest. Such tasks, at certain times of the rural year, took precedence over schooling, especially when school fees were tuppence every week!

In addition, health concerns would encourage absence. This was an age when illnesses such as scarlet fever, measles and whooping cough were potentially fatal for children and a crowded classroom was a hot-house for germs. In very wet or cold weather, attendance rates would plummet as parents sought to protect their offspring.

In the 1870s, however, matters improved. A national debate around the slogan "Education for All" was heating up, and was reflected in the expansion of the village school with the building of a second classroom. During the next decade prizes were awarded for good attendance and fees for the paupers paid from the poor rate.

A major step forward came with the passing of Lord Sandon's 1876 Elementary Education Act, which declared all children should receive that first important stage of learning. Then in 1880, the sentiment was reinforced by making education compulsory up the age of ten. Finally, in 1891, the real breakthrough occurred with the Education Act of that year which made elementary education free, individual fees being replaced by state grants. From then on the budding scholars and unwilling students alike of St Ippolyts had no excuse for absenting themselves from school.

In the meantime, the problem of teacher turnover continued. No less than six came and went in just five years during the 1890s. The picturesque setting of the school clearly didn't make up for the challenges presented by the down-to-earth young yokels.

Nevertheless, with the arrival of Joseph (Joe) Cole and his wife in September 1891, the situation was resolved. The couple settled in well and spent the rest of their working lives in St Ippolyts. With a love of strict discipline, learning and sport in equal measures, Joe Cole became a legend in the district. In the 1930s, still going strong, he taught this writer's father, who spoke of his old teacher with great respect and just a hint of affection.

Chapter Fourteen
Bandits on the Beach

It was close to heaven. Those first days of the summer holiday after breaking up from school were idyllic. Just to think: no school, no homework, no responsibilities, no worries, for many, many weeks into the far distant future. Summer stretched out before us, endlessly languid, warm, golden and light. No need to get up early or to come home early, for the evenings extended beyond bedtime and the outside beckoned for play beyond dusk.

We could just lie, for what seemed hours, in the new-mown grass of the recreation ground, having fought a battle with the freshly cut clippings, exhausted in the heat, staring at the blue sky. It always seemed to be blue, apart from the occasional interloper of an unravelling cloud. Occasionally, more eye-catching, a soundless jet would crawl across the perfect surface, cutting a straight line, leaving a pencil trail of vapour. It was enough to watch that trace gradually dissipate, growing wider and fainter until it finally blended into the ether again. Would surely be a fighter, we would think, flown by some heroic pilot.

There was much idleness to look forward to and savour in the summer weeks ahead. Lazy days lounging in front of the TV, following the ritual of Wimbledon, hoping against hope that the latest English champion would proceed

162

beyond the early rounds. Then becoming absorbed by the American and Australian stars who inevitably dominated the tournament. They didn't have the style or sporting characteristics of our British heroes, but, as the BBC commentators had to remind us in their polished tones, one had to admire their energy and single-mindedness, even if their consistent ability to win was slightly uncouth.

Cricket also played its part in defining those restful weeks. Like summer, each test match was played out against a backdrop of drowsy heat, punctuated by fitful showers or downpours, which interrupted play and affected results. How glorious to have the luxury to follow an entire five-day test match on the radio. We anxiously tracked the play against the old enemy Australia, or the swashbuckling West Indians, who clearly hadn't been coached properly in the forward defensive shot. Even the games that resulted in draws were exciting to us junior experts, who filled in entire score sheets and argued over the effectiveness of obscure cricket shots, fielding placements and bowling techniques.

Some days, when the heat bore down, we were allowed an expedition to the local town swimming pool. Off I would set on the local bus, with a couple of friends, swimming costume rolled in a towel and carried in a duffle bag – two shillings in my pocket. Nine pence the bus fare each way and sixpence left over for a drink or snack. Hours spent in the crowded pool, swimming, diving, bombing or playing football on the grass. Then spending the return bus fare on another bag of crisps or cup of hot Oxo – sheer luxury. The consequence was a weary, three-mile walk home along the Gosmore lane, to arrive home stinking of chlorine, eyes bleary-red and ears waterlogged. But it was worth it.

This was summer in the life of the village; like a warm bath enveloping you. The highlight was yet to come. As the days ticked by, our anticipation grew, for my family always saved the best till last. Because of Dad's job, and something to do with the cost of it, our family holiday always took place during the last two weeks of the school summer break.

Our regular destination in those years was the Norfolk coast, on account of its accessibility and some tenuous family connection that I never really grasped. Favourite location was the village of Hemsby, a few miles from the kiss-me-quick commercialisation of Yarmouth, Norfolk's Blackpool. Hemsby was quieter, less spoiled, offering miles of sand dunes and soft sandy beaches.

We had tried Devon one year and I remembered the small coves overhung with huge cliffs and the villages on Dartmoor steeped in fairy and pixie lore, crudely translated into tourist bric-a-brac. But Devon was so far, and my father had numerous stress attacks driving there through interminable traffic jams. My mother panicked over the road maps and they irritated each other. Who needed Devon when for us children Hemsby was perfect? It offered everything necessary – sand, sea, swimming, one-armed bandits, ice cream and fish and chips; but above all, freedom and adventure.

For my parents, the whole exercise was a trial. Booking accommodation was by letter only. Liaising with relatives, who may join or visit us while there was complicated. Organising my elder sister, younger brother and me, who were willing to help but more of a hindrance, was a chore. My mother, ever kind and unsure of her own ability, fretting over the packing. What was needed? Surely, she would forget something, while my father harassed her to get things ready, as he became increasingly anxious at the prospect of the journey.

Finally, suitcases and holdalls were stuffed with clothing and all the paraphernalia of a summer holiday. Everything was to be taken with us. We did not pay for things once we were there, apart from food. Nevertheless, we took all our nourishment for the journey itself and many additional supplies. You did not stop at cafes on the way, for this would entail extra expense and delay. No, all victuals were packed in plastic containers and bags.

Ham and egg sandwiches featured as the staple sustenance. These were embellished by boiled eggs, tomatoes and sausage rolls. Apples and oranges provided the dessert and, inevitably, bags of boiled sweets to keep us happy on the back seat. For drink, ample thermos flasks would be filled with milky, sweetened tea, and a bottle of lemonade for luxury. A plastic bucket was strategically placed in the back of the van in case of travel sickness or other emergencies. As the day of departure loomed we would be put to bed early in a state of extreme anticipation and joy. We couldn't sleep much of course.

When the day dawned we were aroused early and sleepily piled into the back of the green van along with luggage and nourishment. Dad's first car was a green van of unknown brand and model, with an old bus seat fixed in the back for us children. It had no side windows in the back, which made it dark and breathless. We didn't care, especially when we were going on holiday. There was too much joy to look forward to.

Off we chugged, the engine spluttering and the gears grinding. Only about a hundred and ten miles to go, which should mean a journey of some three hours. Head for Newmarket, get through Thetford, negotiate Norwich and we were virtually there. For Dad, this was agony. He wasn't comfortable driving outside the lanes of North Hertfordshire, but to tackle the highways of Cambridgeshire and Norfolk was like embarking on an expedition into the unknown. It was a test of nerves.

Inevitably, they frayed. They were stretched taut by the long delays at Newmarket, for half the population of Hertfordshire was also headed for the North Sea coast that Saturday. The two lane main roads were not built for traffic like this and every town centre was a bottleneck, creating long tailbacks. Dad crouched over the wheel, sweat running down his forehead.

Meanwhile, Mum cheerily tried to distract the three of us in the dismal recesses of the van. We played "I Spy" endlessly, until we were bored. Then, of course, we quarrelled. I argued with my sister about the games. I teased my younger brother. He was easy meat, on account of his vulnerability to car sickness. A few mock retching sounds, or poking my fingers provocatively down my throat did the trick. He would soon feel ill, and the plastic bucket brought into emergency use.

I would be scolded by my mother, and shouted at by my father. My sister would begin to tease me. I was a baby and spoilt, she would say, with some justification. We were all overheating, and so was the green van. This caused a crisis. Steam issued from the bonnet. Dad pulled over half onto the grass verge. Cars hooted and drivers cursed as they swerved around us. Dad set off swearing in search of water. Mum, bewildered and near tears, ensured us all was well and we would soon be there. I had to get out to go to the toilet, clambering through the hedge at the roadside, highly embarrassed at the thought I could be seen by all the passing traffic.

Finally, on the way again. More delays at Thetford. Time to stop for food and drink and some respite from the tension of the drive. Then we were on the road again to Norwich, a major city for us, another obstacle for Dad, before the final run in to Hemsby. Great relief as we arrived at the village on the coast. Some last minute complications finding the person with the key to our "chalet" and finding our home on the dunes. We had made it.

We were all tired and irritable. My younger brother was asleep. The wooden chalet reminded me of a ranch house in the Wild West. The journey, which had taken seven hours, was over. We would have fish and chips for supper. It couldn't get much better. Everything smelt differently and the air tasted of the sea, which we could hear plunging rhythmically onto the beach barely two hundred yards away over the dunes. We slept well.

Our temporary residence was simple and sparse with none of the luxuries or comforts of home. There was no running hot water, no TV or radio (we brought our own transistor along for the Archers and the cricket scores). No carpets adorned the wooden plank floor, which was always covered in a layer of sand. To no avail our mother tried to get us to brush ourselves down after a day playing in the dunes and on the beach. This minimalism added to the adventure, resembling a comfortable form of camping. We had, after all, proper, if slightly hard, beds.

For Mum, the lack of a fridge or washing machine was not entirely new, but the two-ring stove and deficiency of other household amenities meant that the daily chore of running home and caring for the family continued more or less unabated. At least she didn't have to cook so much. We ate a lot of cereal and sandwiches and salads, and frequent portions of fish and chips, which tasted even better at the seaside.

Our chalet stood right on the dunes, detached and private, the nearest neighbour being fifty yards away. It was five minutes' walk from the simple parade of shops on the main track that led down to the beach. These shops catered to all our basic needs, groceries, household, beachwear and toys, suntan oil and camomile lotion.

Camomile was an integral part of the holiday, as its soothing and healing properties were inevitably called upon from the very second day, when our pale Hertfordshire skins were burnt red raw after playing in the sun the whole day, despite parental warnings. We smelt permanently of suntan cream and camomile lotion and the taste of salt lingered in our mouths. After a few days the skin on our shoulders and backs would begin to blister and itch and then peel off in ragged strips. More camomile and then the procedure of sun burning would begin again.

How could the sun be avoided when the dunes at our doorstep offered such an adventure playground? Here my sister, brother and myself would run between the grassy hillocks, jump and roll down the slopes, dig tunnels to Australia, half bury each other, or just lie on the warm sand. We would play there for hours, unattended, within shouting reach of home. No-one was concerned for our safety and no-one bothered us.

Occasionally, we would wander down to the shops, all wooden and set on a stretch of planked decking some sixty yards long, lifted from the sandy track. At its outer edge ran a railing, about waist high to an adult. This gave the place the air of a town in a Western film. Here was the saloon, here the sheriff's office and here the hardware store. The handrail was where the drifters and hired guns tethered their horses before crashing through the swing doors to confront their foes in a gunfight.

To help the imagination along Hemsby had its own gunslinger. He was always there, outside the parade of shops. A fully dressed cowboy, with wide brimmed hat, chequered red shirt, tassels on the sleeves, gauchos and boots. Most intriguing of all he sported a real cowboy gun belt with two holsters and realistic looking plastic six guns.

We called him "the Bandit". He was older than us, probably in his late teens, and was, as Dad described it "missing something up top". Nevertheless, he was always ready for a gunfight. If you pretended to shoot at him, with two fingers pointed, he would be quick on the draw with his six guns, blazing back. Ducking behind the inflatable rubber rings and lilos hung in front of the shops, he would peer round and pretend to ambush you. We never spoke to him and I never heard him utter a word. He was quite harmless, though we were told not to get too close to him. I always thought he was protecting his row of shops from outlaws.

Most days, as long as it wasn't raining, we spent hours together as a family on the beach. It was never very crowded, and we took wind breaks with us to shield us from the cool breeze which regularly swept in over the North Sea. The adults would sit and talk, read magazines and enjoy a picnic, while we played endlessly on the water line. We spent hours building pointless sand defences against the incoming tide, and like King Canute suffering inevitable defeat.

Swimming in the cold water needed determination, particularly the first immersion. Once in, we could enjoy the crashing waves, leaping over and diving through them, until we were frozen and salt-encrusted. We never seemed to think of safety, as we frolicked under the casual observation of our parents. It was time eventually to go back to the beach, shivering and huddled in towels, for hot tea from the thermos.

On the occasional wet days, the time dragged interminably. Confined to the chalet, we would be visited by Uncle Charlie and Auntie Eva with their sons, David and Stephen. The adults seemed to enjoy the enforced idleness and spent hours playing cards, sipping beer and talking. The inactivity depressed me. I could only play cards or Monopoly for so long, without being able to run around.

Relief came in the form of being given a shilling in penny coins and told to go off to the amusement arcades. This was better – with my sister, brother and two cousins we would head off to the shelter and glitzy attractions of the arcades, clutching our twelve precious coins. Amid the noise – the rock and roll background music, the bells and thuds of the pin balls machines, rattle of coins when the slot machines paid out – we would enjoy the success and disappointments of the gambler. Our main adversaries were the one-armed bandits, rows upon rows of them, artfully designed to gobble up our precious assets, while tempting us to continue with the occasional paltry win staving off the ineluctable bankruptcy.

Nevertheless, we firmly believed that a certain skill was at play. You had to identify the bandits that paid out more often. You had to linger behind someone playing and leap in if they abandoned the effort after a significant number of failures. When all your coins were finally spent the only recourse was to hang around the arcade to see if someone would forget to collect all their winnings from the bandits' trays, or by mistake leave the machine with one pull of the lever unused.

Some evenings were passed down the local pub. Mum, Dad, Uncle Charlie and Auntie Eva would meet up with scarcely known relatives, distant cousins of Norfolk extraction, who were of little interest to me as their children were far too young to be of any consequence or to be playfellows.

Early in the evening, bribed with lemonade and crisps, we would enjoy the garden, but as the hours dragged by and darkness began to fall, we would become bored. Further bribery would come in the form of more drinks and sometimes, as a special treat, sixpence to go to the nearest fish and chip shop for a bag of chips, or a tub of mushy peas. The adults talked and drank inside, but we weren't allowed in and had to wait outside.

On one day at least during our stay we would visit Yarmouth for a day out. Compared to quaint, dozy Hemsby, Yarmouth was a metropolis for holiday makers. Full of crowds, colour, noise and entertainments of all kinds the town delivered a raucous impression. Rows of shops, arcades, amusements, cafes and pubs stretched for miles along the seafront. The pier offered further entertainment, along with exotic food stalls offering cockles, mussels and whelks. Smells that were exotic to me – a mingling of salt-laden air, seafood, deep-fried batter, the sweet sickliness of candy-floss and ubiquitous tobacco.

That's where the stranger spoke to me once. Waiting on the promenade, while Mum and Dad took the others to the toilet, I leaned on the railings enjoying the sunshine and fresh breeze, watching the waves crash repetitively into white foam and the swimmers screaming with joy as they jumped to avoid them. I wished I was there with them, not walking about and shopping.

He leaned on the railings next to me and seemed very friendly. "What's your name," he asked, and when I told him he followed up with more questions. He was grown up but not very old. I didn't mind him talking to me, and I was not worried, but I thought it was odd that he would bother to talk to me.

After a few minutes he offered to buy me an ice cream, but I said no, because I was waiting for my parents.

"They'll be back any minute," I said, in a calculated way to see if he would hang around.

"Right," he said quickly, "Well, have a nice holiday", and then he was gone, walking briskly away and not looking round.

I told Mum and Dad about him, when they came back. Dad looked annoyed and asked me if I could still see him, but he had disappeared into the crowds. They told me, as they had often before, that I shouldn't talk to strangers. I knew this well enough because I had learnt about kidnappings and murders on the TV. But the stranger who addressed me was quite harmless I thought, and there were lots of people around. I wasn't at all afraid of him.

Eventually, our two-week idyll would draw to an end, after what seemed like an age of self-indulgence and freedom. Returning home required its own rituals, such as buying gifts for friends and relatives – cheap, tacky, throwaway gifts from the souvenir shops. A tea towel imprinted with a picture of the Yarmouth seafront for Auntie Brenda; a set of cork table maps with a design of coastline of Norfolk; a wooden ash tray with a Hemsby inscription for Dad's workmate, and so on.

For the children, the choosing of presents for our friends was straightforward, for the favoured few would receive a dentally threatening stick of rock – essentially a cylinder of concentrated sugar. Red on the outside, with a white interior, the eight-inch long destroyer of tooth enamel would have the name of Hemsby running through it centre, so we would not forget where we purchased it as we slurped our way greedily through it.

Normally two days before we set off home, with barely enough time for the Post Office to do its duty, we would remember to send postcards. The adults would enjoy selecting the saucy ones, giggling conspiratorially, while handling us the ones with scenes of Hemsby for our friends. Personally, I didn't find the cards funny. What was humorous about a fat man in a swimming costume looking for his little boy, who is out of sight underneath his overhanging belly, saying "I can't see my little Willy."?

Once the postcards had been sent, however, and the presents selected, the dreaded day of departure loomed. Did the weather really deteriorate in the last two days? Or was it merely our mood that became overcast and dismal. The wind picked up, the temperature dropped and it sometimes drizzled. It was, after all, well into September and autumn was elbowing summer out of the way.

Driving home, the gloom deepened. In contrast to the mischievous behaviour of the outward trip, we sat largely in silence, suffering from the itchiness of our fast-disappearing sunburn and the disagreeable thought of having to go back to school. Similarly, our parents spoke little, preoccupied with thoughts of family duties and, in my father's case, a return to the rounds of house-to-house insurance selling and premiums collecting.

We retraced our steps through the traffic bottlenecks of Norfolk, Cambridgeshire and Hertfordshire. We would sleep much of the way. When we finally reached our village and drew up outside our house, it seemed peculiarly cold, dark and alien.

But once inside, with a roaring fire warming the living room, having unpacked and shaken the sand from our clothes, and taking a stick of rock to suck on as we huddled around the TV for children's hour, it didn't seem quite so bad. Holidays were interludes of escapism and freedom, but Hemsby wasn't a real place to live in, like our village. It couldn't offer the same comfort and security, though a bandit or two would have been a welcome distraction sometimes.

Chapter Fifteen
Riot and Dissent

The good folk of St Ippolyts and Gosmore were generally god-fearing and law-abiding over the years, with the great tremors and wars of the outside world only intermittently impinging on their tranquil rural lives. Apart from a few landowning families and a handful of farmers, the villagers eked out a subsistence standard of living from farm labouring and basic handicrafts. Up to the twentieth century life was primitive, as they sought to bring up their families in rudimentary cottages, with little comfort or entertainment.

Nevertheless, they were not completely cut off from the great happenings and movements of history and every so often we find the locals responding to external events – and not always in a compliant manner.

As early as 1666, for example, following the disastrous outbreak of the Great Fire of London, County Records reveal an obstinate streak in one local. The fire caused considerable disquiet for many miles around the city. From Hitchin and St Ippolyts the glow of the conflagration could be clearly seen in the sky and there were serious concerns that the Armageddon could spread as far as the local area.

As a result, citizens were summoned by the Town Constable of Hitchin to do their part in keeping watch and preparing to help beat out any encroaching flames. Unfortunately, one Elizabeth Warland of St Ippolyts, who lived on the main London Road, didn't feel inclined to take this seriously and failed to respond. Consequently, a few months later, she was hauled before the authorities and fined "for refusing to watch at the constable's request when the fire was in London." A little harsh, given the fire was some thirty miles away!

Throughout the 18th century calm generally prevailed, with little noticeable disruption to the seasonal grind of farm work. Villagers were, however, infected by the spirit of dissenting, which proved popular in the environs of Hitchin. In 1705, a Baptist meeting house was opened in St Ippolyts in the home of one John Needham, while the Congregationalist church in Hitchin recorded four members coming from the village. This did not go down well with the parish Church of England vicars, who regularly complained about the spread of these radical ideas and the absence from their services they caused.

If religion offered the serious face of dissent, football gave vent to a more riotous form of misbehaviour. From Elizabethan times the game was popular but generally frowned upon for the mob violence it engendered. It was, explained one Elizabethan writer "a friendlie kind of fyghte rather than a play or recreation."

The problem was there weren't really any rules in those days, nor any limit to the number of people taking part. Consequently, the entire male population of villages would enthusiastically aim to get the ball – usually a pig's bladder – over the line or through the goal of the opposition. The result was a mass brawl and many injuries.

In 1775 the village of Gosmore took on their larger neighbours Hitchin. We read of "a great football match taking place." It obviously extended over several miles.

The ball "drowned for a time in Priory pond, forced on Angel Street, across the Market Place and final goaled in the porch of St Mary's."

Interesting that Hitchin's fine church and holy place was the chosen goal for the contest. Notable also that the village yobbos seem to have been just too much for the more refined townies.

Like the rest of the country the local citizenry would have been pre-occupied by the threat of Napoleon in the early years of the 19th century and it seems a couple of village lads joined the army and lived to tell the tale.

The immediate effect of the Little Emperor's grand ambitions on the farm labourers of the village was to depress agriculture, along with job opportunities and wages. By 1815, as the French bogeyman was bundled off to St Helena to end his days in solitude, the situation for the working man was made even more dire by the increasing enforcement of Enclosure Acts.

This aspect of the agricultural revolution led to greater output and efficiency in the long run. However, by consolidating the lands of the wealthier farmers, and by encroaching on traditional rights of common land and foraging, enclosures meant less demand for labour, restricted access to land and livestock, and even greater hardship for the labouring classes.

A "Petition to Enclose" in St Ippolyts and its surroundings was posted on the church door in 1810. A year later the plans gained Royal Assent, having swiftly passed through the necessary parliamentary process. Measures to carve up the common land, formerly shared by the villagers, and the hedging and fencing of private farm land proceeded without pause. Following a poor harvest in 1813 more and more were cast into poverty.

Unsurprisingly, desperate people took matters into their own hands and at Easter, 1815, frustration boiled over into a full-scale riot in the parish. Seventeen villagers, led by a certain Thomas Hickson, caused a major commotion, demanding work and better wages. Eventually, the fracas was contained and Hickson arrested by the constable. Fortunately, no-one had been seriously injured, nor damage done, but when Hickson appeared before the County Court in Hertford, he was still bound over for a year and fined £40, which was a stiff punishment for a manual worker earning a few shillings a week.

In the context of the penal code of the time, Hickson got off fairly lightly. In contrast, in the mid-1820s, a couple of village ne'er-do-wells were to feel the full force of establishment vindictiveness. Local brothers William and James Castle hatched a plot to steal the copper cauldron used for brewing at the manor house of St Ibbs. Not an easy task to liberate the bulky and heavy container, but worth it if its value of 20 shillings could be realised! They nearly succeeded, secretively seizing their booty from the coach house and scarpering off to the nearby Hertfordshire town of Ware.

Unluckily for them, the head butler of the manor house, Francis Best, was both diligent and astute. Having made his enquiries, Best tracked the miserable brothers down in Ware, reclaimed the vessel and cast the lads onto the mercy of the courts. Regrettably for them, mercy was in short supply. They were condemned to seven years' transportation to Australia. Thrown into Hertford gaol, they would have been subjected to the treadmill, and then, most likely, packed off to the rotting hulks in the Thames Estuary that served as temporary holding prisons, before being shipped across to the other side of the world. Sadly, they never returned to their tranquil village.

Further widespread agricultural disturbances flared up in the 1830s, as increasing mechanisation, particularly the use of threshing machines, threatened jobs and livelihoods. There were frequent outbreaks of rick-burning, machine smashing and menacing of farmers and landowners throughout the South of England. These outbursts were known as the "Swing Riots" because anonymous letters to farmers promising dire consequences were signed "Captain Swing", bearing the unsubtle warning of lynching.

St Ippolyts didn't remain untouched. In December, 1830, 24 village sturdies volunteered as Special Constables in response to a direct appeal to the country by a shaken Prime Minister Lord Melbourne. Frustrations came to a head locally the following year, when a riot took place involving some dozen labourers. Once it was suppressed, six of the participants were arraigned before Hertford Quarter Sessions. William Slater, identified as the instigator, was sentenced to one month's imprisonment, while the others were sent down for two weeks. All were condemned to hard labour. At least they avoided transportation.

Following the period of reform in the 1830s, the next decade began to see some marginal improvement in the prospects of the working poor. Two major factors were the Repeal of the Corn Laws in 1846 and the advent of railways. Corn Law reform meant that cheaper foreign corn was allowed into the country, so the price of bread dropped dramatically, and living standards therefore rose. At the same time, the building of the railways meant plenty of

179

alternative manual work became available. Railways also offered much greater mobility in the search for jobs. Neither change helped farmers much, especially the smaller ones, and the next decades witnessed a growing number of farmers in difficulty.

In terms of maintaining civil order the formation of the Hitchin Police Force in 1841 ushered in a new era. Recruitment was encouraged by the offer of the generous wages of 19 shillings a week.

Shortly after they seemed to have suffered from an excess of zeal. We read in the local court records: "Freeman King, Frederick King and Herbert Saunders, labourers of Gosmore, were charged with making a bonfire in the middle of the road at Gosmore. PC Perry put it out…"

Given that it was Guy Fawkes night, and given that villagers traditionally built bonfires on the roads, PC Perry was being over-officious in the discharge of his duty. Perhaps he needed to prove he was worth his 19 shillings.

The decade ended on a tragic note, with at least twenty villagers dying of cholera in 1849, as the pestilence swept its deadly way through the unsanitary and overcrowded cottages of the poor.

Overall, however, cheaper bread, more construction and industrial employment and greater mobility led to better conditions for working people, though farmers suffered from the impact of imported products and greater competition from industry. During the 1870s and 1880s we see in local records an increased turnover in the sales of farms, stock and equipment.

By this time agricultural workers were also beginning to assert themselves politically. In 1873 the famous activist Joseph Arch, who was to form the National Union of Agricultural Labourers the following year, hosted a mass meeting on Butts Close in nearby Hitchin. More than a thousand people showed up to hear him speak, and we can be sure that at least a handful of St Ippolyts working men were counted among their number.

Finally, in 1885, the suffrage was extended to all men, regardless of their economic standing, and the village labourer could finally play his part in the democratic process. In the same year, hopeful candidates from both the Conservative and Liberal Parties made their way to the school house in St Ippolyts in an attempt to sway the newly enfranchised local voters their way.

Despite this constitutional outlet for protest, grievances against farmers continued through the 1880s. The main cause usually being the employers' attempts to cut wages in the face of falling product prices. In St Ippolyts and Gosmore this normally took the form of hay ricks being deliberately set on fire – an alarmingly frequent occurrence.

In October 1881, a large barley rick was set aflame on a local farm and then a hay stack later the same day. Suspicion of arson fell upon eighteen-year-old William Dear, who had reason for revenge. He had recently been sacked from this farm for neglecting his duty and letting a herd of cows in his care wander off. William was arrested, but due to lack of evidence, he was acquitted two months later.

In the same year a near disastrous conflagration occurred at Lodge's Farm. Tenant farmer Gates had left for Hitchin market leaving his fourteen-year-old daughter in charge. Somehow fire broke out. The girl, the other children and the farmhouse itself were saved, thanks to the speedy reactions of the Hitchin Fire Brigade. Most striking, however, is the lack of co-operation they received from the local hoodlums, who, according to reports, pelted the fireman with onions while they bravely fought the fire.

Was this because they had a grudge against farmer Lodge, or simply because they were ruffians and drunk? Whatever the background, the village reputation for roughness, dating back to the football match of the previous century, had clearly not been refined. Similarly, its tradition of religious dissent continued, with significant numbers of villagers following Baptist and Congregationalist tendencies.

By the turn of the century, life in many respects had improved. Religious and political freedoms had been established, working and domestic conditions ameliorated, educational opportunities increased and advances in medicine ensured healthier lives.

The villagers of St Ippolyts would have shared in the sense of well-being and international supremacy that late Victorian Britain enjoyed. Like the rest of the country they would also have to face up to the tragedies and heartbreak that loomed in the coming decades.

Chapter Sixteen
Alfie Turner

The Great War took a terrible toll on the young men of the parish, as it did of so many communities throughout the country. No fewer than twenty names are listed on the memorial to commemorate the victims of that cruel conflict. Virtually one in four of the village men of military age perished. Family names familiar to the village – Amos, Chalkley, Isaacs, Turners among them – lost their sons, in the prime of life, consumed in the titanic struggles of northern France and Belgium.

World War Two inflicted similar sacrifices. Six villagers, in their late teens or twenties, were lost, and the record of their deaths on the same monument next to the parish church tragically resonates with some of the great battles of the war. Air Gunner Hubert Clark – killed in action at El Alamein; Flight Lt. Brian McMaster – killed in action; Lt. Duncan McMurtrie – killed at Anzio; Able Seaman Harold O'Dell – lost in the sinking of HMS Ajax; Private Roland Willis – killed in action; and Gunner Alfred Charles Turner – died in captivity.

Every one of these is a story of equal loss and grief for their families and the village, but the fate of Alfred Turner is particularly poignant. The Turners lived barely a few hundred yards from the home where I grew up and whenever I passed by as a boy I couldn't help but think, with a shiver, of his sad end. Alfred, or "Alfie", as he was known to all, was a class mate and team mate of my father. I see him, sitting upright and proud in the 1932 photo of the school football team – looking slightly quizzical and frailer than many of the boys. My father had told me about him and his death as a prisoner of war at the hands of the Japanese, whose treatment of their captives had been fully revealed at the war's end and was a source of much bitterness and resentment.

He may not have been as physically robust as some of his contemporaries, but Alfie didn't lack courage. Even before the war, or conscription, had started, he patriotically joined the Territorial Army, probably in 1938. This part-time citizen defence force taught him the basics of soldiering. Signing up to the Herts Yeomanry, he became an artillery man, Bombardier or Gunner Turner.

Having been formed in 1794, in response to the threat posed by the French Revolution, the Hertfordshire Yeomanry had a long history. After serving in the Boer War and the First World War, the regiment became part of the Royal Artillery in the inter-war years. On the outbreak of war in September 1939, Alfie found himself assigned to the 344 Hitchin Battery, and a member of the regular army, in the Royal Artillery.

For the next two years he was to remain out of harm's way. As the phoney war in Europe dragged on and as the Battle of Britain was being fought in the skies, he was posted to Macclesfield and then to Sheringham to continue his training. Months later, as the disasters of the 1940 France campaign unfolded, and culminated in the "glorious" defeat of Dunkirk, Alfie stayed with his regiment in the UK.

All was to change in 1941. In this bleakest of war years for Britain, when all seemed lost in Europe, the Japanese military machine launched its ferocious assault on colonial interests in the Far East. As part of the response, the Herts Yeomanry was packed off to India to join the 18th Infantry Division in readiness to defend the Empire. Alfie suddenly had to adapt to entirely alien environments.

By the end of 1941 the Japanese armies had battered the British outpost of Hong Kong into submission. Their troops had over-run Indo-China and were pouring across the Irrawaddy and Salween rivers into Burma, brushing aside brave but ineffective resistance. Soon they were moving up to the very border of India and hurtling down the peninsula of Malaysia. The advance was aimed like a javelin at the heart of British imperial power in the region, the fortress island of Singapore.

Singapore would surely hold out. It had massive artillery defences. It was well defended with substantial forces. So the British thought. To make sure, additional reserves were hastily sent to repel the Japanese progress, among them the 18th Division, including the Hitchin Battery, and Alfie.

By the end of January in the new year, 1942, the 18th was in Malaysia, but in steady retreat south as the Japanese, using swift movement and superior jungle warfare techniques, outmanoeuvred the British forces. Across the narrow straits that divide the island of Singapore from Malaysia, the 18th made one last stubborn stand at Johor Bahru, before pulling back to the island itself.

Even then the British had reason to be confident. Singapore was defended by 85,000 troops, against the besieging enemy's 30,000, who were operating on extended supply lines. Churchill, desperate to avoid further military humiliation, harangued Generals Wavell and Percival, the unfortunate men in charge, with orders to fight to the last bullet.

Posted to the northeast of the island, to defend the Semarang naval base area, the 18th Division took up positions on the coast. The men must have awaited the onslaught nervously for Perceval expected the attack to be centred on this strategic point. It was not to be, however. Once again the Japanese proved themselves smarter in tactics and surprise and after five days' relentless air and artillery bombardment, stormed over the straits on February 8th against weaker forces to the west of the island.

Chaos ensued. Perceval's response was indecisive. Amid the confusion the 18th Division was ordered inland on February 12th to defend the reservoirs and assist in a counterattack. It was all too late.

Pressured by the lack of ammunition and water, and concerned for the safety of the civilian population, Perceval surrendered. In so doing he handed Alfie Turner and more than 85,000 British and Commonwealth troops over to the Japanese. Most had hardly been able to fire a shot in the battle.

Initially, they were herded into a prison camp adjacent to Changi prison in Singapore, a facility designed for a fraction of their number. Overcrowded and poorly fed – the Japanese had made no preparations for dealing with such a large number of prisoners – they were soon suffering from heat and disease.

Little did they know that their agony had barely begun. By the early Autumn of 1942 the Japanese started trucking them north, into Burma and Thailand, to work as slave labour on the notorious "Death Railway".

Alfie, along with the others of the 18th, were packed into cramped rice wagons, thirty men at a time, and made to endure an horrendous three-day, four-night journey, with insufficient food and water. At the end of the line, they were force marched for many hours more to a place called Tamarkan in Thailand. Here they were made to build their own prison camp consisting of primitive bamboo huts.

Started in October, 1942, the infamous railway project was to take a year to build. The allied prisoners, along with many Asian labourers, were compelled to work in insufferable conditions. Without adequate food, medicine and rest, they were forced to undertake heavy manual work for twelve hours a day under a brutal regime. Unsurprisingly, they were vulnerable to tropical diseases.

Those based at Tamarkan were relatively lucky. Under the heroic leadership of Lieutenant Colonel Philip Toosey of the 18th Division, who bravely negotiated where he could with the camp authorities, they at least had a sense of leadership and hope. They had clean water and hygiene was maintained as far as possible. As a result, the two thousand five hundred of those captured who were based at Tamarkan avoided the ravages of cholera that affected camps further up the line in 1943.

Sadly, it was not enough to save Alfie. The twenty-four-year-old villager, who must have wondered why fate was putting him through such an ordeal, died in November, 1943. Poignantly, it was a month after the main line was finished.

Alfie died at the hospital set up by the prisoners at Chungkai, not far from the camp. We don't know what killed him. It may have been dysentery, malaria or beriberi, or another disease that flourished in weakened, undernourished bodies. Perhaps, like many others, his spirit was broken after a year and nine months of captivity and he simply lost the will to carry on.

He lies in the neatly kept war cemetery at Chungkai, along with over 1,700 other Allied victims, a world away from the Hertfordshire village which mourned him in respectful tones for many years after.

Chapter Seventeen
Changes

Life had a reassuring permanence for the first decade of my life. People and places were immutable, fixed in time and space. I was increasingly aware of my own physical growth, and that of my peers, but my environment was like an unmoving backdrop against which the evolving stages of life were enacted. Village society was unerringly benign. We were sheltered from the troubles of the world. Time crept by unnoticed. Summer holidays lasted for ever, as did school terms.

However, in my twelfth year,1961, this unquestioned continuity would be shattered in a number of ways. Habits of life taken for granted would be altered and unknown situations and threats present themselves.

Not least among these was the inevitable wrench of leaving the family atmosphere of St Ippolyts Primary School and having to deal with the daunting prospect of attending the Boys' Grammar School in our local town, Hitchin. It was a yearly ritual, of which I was fully aware, that two or three boys from our village school would be "selected" by the Eleven Plus exam to attend this prestigious establishment and be moulded for success in the world. The remainder would be packed off to the secondary modern school, named after the town's famous son, Henry

Bessemer, where they would be taught basic literacy and numeracy in preparation for joining the workforce at fifteen.

My sister Sue, two years older, already attended the Girls' Grammar School, becoming only the second Wingate in our family branch ever to attend grammar school. Our Aunt Audrey (actually our cousin) had been the first, so achieving unique career status by becoming a white collar professional as a tax official. Sue was doing well. She was very clever and even liked reading books!

These precedents, however, did not make my fate any less challenging. There was the expectation to cope with first. Mum and Dad, who had never been too demanding in these respects, were nevertheless extremely proud and Dad already voiced dreams of me becoming a lawyer, financier, or even a civil servant of high standing. But would I cope with the academic demands of the school? You had to study different subjects there, disciplines that sounded strange and complicated, like Chemistry and Latin. I wouldn't be competing with the village boys and girls any more but with town boys, who were sons of doctors and professors and bankers. Homework would have to be done every single night. The teachers wouldn't be maternal, like Miss Austin, or kind, like Mr Livingstone, but strict and demanding. They caned the boys who misbehaved or failed to work hard enough! Even worse I would have to play new sports, such as rugby and hockey, when football was my passion.

Socially also, this would cause disruption. Only Peter Dawson, the son of a local farming family, was selected along with me to go to the grammar school. He was likeable, but not a close friend. All my friends were going to the Bessemer and I envied them the fact they would have companionship from day one. I, on the other hand, would have to start entirely on my own. Even Peter Dawson would not be in the same class in form one. Adding to this problem would be the stigma attached to grammar school status. While not manifesting itself in outright hostility, it meant I would henceforth be labelled a snob among my peers. Meanwhile, I would have to deal with those smart and wealthy town boys, who would no doubt look down on a villager.

The grammar school was a seemingly huge institution, with over 600 boys. Instead of being a leading pupil, I would become a minnow overnight, thrown into an unforgiving sea with plenty of hostile predators around. As the youngest there, new boys would be at the mercy of the older ones, the prefects and bullies, especially those from year two, maliciously celebrating the fact that they were no longer the novices. Rumours came to us of initiation rites, of duckings and inkings. This is what I faced. It would be a trial.

Even the practicalities were challenging. I would have to get to town, with my sister, on the Bedford bus, taking a fifteen-minute ride. And then get home again. The buses only ran once an hour, so timing would be all important. As I had rarely been to Hitchin on my own, this commute was worrying. All this to be overcome, carrying a satchel full of books and a duffel bag full of games kit. Life was set to become burdensome indeed.

It wasn't easy for Mum either. Not only did I have to be kitted out in full school uniform comprising shorts, shirt, tie, pullovers, socks, blazer, two sets of games kit, and even a cap, all of which had to be individually labelled with sown-in name tags.

These domestic preoccupations took place in a year when the world was making its first intrusions into my consciousness.

At the beginning of the year the whole family sat glued to our black and white TV to watch the inauguration of the new President of the United States. Why should this distant political event be of any interest? Mainly because John F Kennedy and his wife were as glamorous as any film star of the age. I didn't pay much attention to these great affairs, but Kennedy's assumption to the Presidency was different, because it was much discussed at school, at home, and around the village. He was young, good looking and an inspiring speaker. I was old enough to recognise this. How much more attractive he was than the old men who ran Britain! Winston Churchill and Harold McMillan were very stuffy in comparison.

But the adults' talk suggested something else – a change in leadership that might ease the Cold War and the dangers of nuclear conflict. We could sense optimism and growing hope that this President would mean a safer and more peaceful world.

In April of that year another TV event captured our imaginations and prompted much talk. The first man had been launched into space! Russian cosmonaut Yuri Gagarin won his place in history by surviving a single orbit of earth. Once again the grainy TV pictures mesmerised us as we watched his heroic welcome home. This was an occasion for more mixed responses, however. Everyone was fascinated with the idea that man had finally reached space. This was a great achievement and it unleashed a torrent of speculation about the next steps in conquering the universe. Soon we would land on the moon, and then Mars, and then…?

Such positive thinking about human progress was tempered by the disturbing realisation that the Russians had succeeded first. Why hadn't Britain, whose heroes, after all, had been the first to climb Everest, to run the first four-minute mile and nearly reach the South Pole, been the first country in space? Or if not Britain, why not our allies the Americans?

This clearly troubled the new President, for Kennedy was soon on the TV again, outlining the USA's determination to regain the lead in space technology. The "Space Race" was on and the US declared its intention to be the first to plant its flag on the dusty surface of the moon. For boys my age this provoked a great deal of interest in space ships, astronauts and rockets. Models of the latter became as popular as Second World War fighter planes.

Also in the background came the news of troubles with Cuba. We had heard of the successful revolution there and of the overthrow of the dictator by Fidel Castro. Now we learnt that some Cubans, backed by the Americans, had tried to capture the island back, by invading with a small army. Castro defeated it and declared that America was an enemy and that he would seek friendship with Russia and Kruschev instead! Everyone thought this was very dangerous, as Cuba lay very close to America and the Cold War became even colder.

If news of world events was intrusive, family gossip was more shocking. Perhaps I was just reaching an age when I paid greater attention to adult chatter, or found it more intriguing, or simply understood it better. Nevertheless, growing awareness that our extended family was not the perfect set of human beings it had seemed, was perturbing. Other families had their problems, particularly those on TV, but our family was surely unblemished. Now I was losing that innocence about matters adult.

The fate of my fathers' sisters was tragic, but rarely spoken about openly. One was burnt alive when her nightdress caught fire as she stood by the open grate. Her child, who became known to us as "Auntie Audrey" was brought up by Dad's eldest brother in the village. She became a good friend and supporter of my mother and helped looked after us when Mum was busy or overstressed. But even Auntie Audrey would not speak about her mother. A mist of silence descended on the adults when we asked our sensation seeking questions about this horrendous incident. It was troubling at this time, to find out a little about the tragedy, but not enough to satisfy our curiosity.

Concerning the other sister, information was equally scant. We wondered why we never met, let alone visited, Aunt Lil, who only lived in Luton, eight miles away. She could have been a source of additional birthday and Christmas presents. Interrogating my mother – certainly not my father, who refused to say anything about it – I found that she had been banished from the family for having a baby. This didn't seem a problem to me, but I vaguely understood that she had not been married and this constituted a problem. What I couldn't understand was that we didn't see her at all, or that we didn't know our cousin. These sensitive adult problems, which made my parents alternately taciturn or embarrassed, made no sense. Was this what growing up meant?

We even learnt that Uncle Ray and Auntie Pearl were not married! How could this be? They were uncle and auntie, so must be married. But no, we heard the story of Auntie Pearl's first marriage in Scotland and how her husband had been aggressive and beaten her. So she left and Uncle Ray came to the rescue. They had been together many years, certainly as long as I was aware of them. I couldn't quite grasp why they hadn't got married, but I wasn't really shocked. We were made to understand that this was something we shouldn't talk about, especially with people outside the family.

As I slowly became aware of these adult problems I recognised that I had to confront them sooner or later. But this was not an enjoyable realisation. I knew I couldn't stop growing up, but that didn't prevent me from holding on to my childhood and hoping it would continue as long as possible.

Further incursions into the comfort zone of childhood came along that year. One took the form of a chilling high profile murder, which created a tremor of discomfort in our family and in the village, because of its proximity. The A6 murder, which was perpetrated just a few miles away, stunned the nation with its callousness. A car driver was shot dead and his female companion raped and shot. She survived, but was paralysed for life. This was the first serious violent crime I was aware of and it made life less secure, to learn such dangerous people as the murderer James Hanratty existed. He was the stuff of nightmares.

Then the Cold War flared up again in October, with a face-to-face confrontation between the USA and the USSR at Checkpoint Charlie in Berlin. American and Russian tanks squared off against each other in one of the most sensitive crises since Cuba. It was headline news around the world and the TV stations covered the situation on a running basis. Nerves were already strained by the building of the Berlin Wall in the preceding months. Checkpoint Charlie remained the key crossing point and therefore focus of tension. For six days Europe held its breath, until an agreement deflated the situation.

Such major international issues were quickly forgotten at my age then, but family matters were more immediate and life-changing. In the early autumn of that year, my parents suddenly announced that we would be expecting a new brother or sister. My sister's, brother's and my reaction to this was positive. It was delightful to think we would have a baby to fuss over and an infant to play with – like a sophisticated toy. It was, nevertheless, also unsettling. Our family of five appeared to be complete. I was eleven, my elder sister thirteen and my younger brother seven. It seemed we didn't need an addition, which might cause imbalance, or attract attention away from us. My parents seemed quite old to have a new baby. And where would it stay? Our small but cosy council house was full with the five of us already.

Preparation for the birth also caused obvious inconvenience. Mum spent a lot of time in bed, resting. As Dad wasn't much use at housework, we were often looked after by Auntie Audrey again. I liked her and her family, so this wasn't a major problem, but it meant we were shuffled between our house and Audrey's, which was a quarter of a mile away at the bottom of Waterdell Lane.

Our new sibling was due in early November, but kept us all waiting. We detected a degree of nervousness among the grown-ups. By November 5th, the baby had still not deigned to make an appearance. Never mind, we had the perfect distraction that evening in Guy Fawkes Night. We trooped down to Audrey's, whose back garden fortunately backed on to the recreation ground where the village bonfire stood in all its grandeur. This was convenient, because Audrey could keep an eye on us and ply us with snacks and fizzy drinks.

Before the evening was over, our relieved and out-of-breath father arrived bearing the good news. We had a little sister and she and our mother were well. That Sally's emergence into the world was hastened by the sound of fireworks is doubtful but made a credible family story.

For the next few nights we three children stayed with our "Aunt" while Mum recuperated. But after a few days we were allowed home and introduced to the latest Wingate, called Sally-Ann. As my father remarked quite accurately, with her rumpled face, puffy eyes and clenched fists, she looked like a miniature prize fighter.

Routines were never quite the same in the household. I was getting used to travelling to Hitchin to attend the grammar school. Mum was pre-occupied with the baby. I was always independent and not one to require much of my mother or demand her attention. As long as she was there to feed, clothe, wash and comfort me I was content. But there was an increasing separation as I went my own way and she cared for the young ones.

However, the greatest surprise of this year of significant change was about to be sprung. Soon after Sally's birth my father announced that we would be moving home!

This really took some absorbing, for we were not going to move to a larger house in St Ippolyts, or indeed a house in Hitchin, but we were relocating a full eight miles away to a village the other side of Hitchin. This seemed like the end of the earth to me. It meant leaving all our friends and familiar surroundings. It meant parting with relatives, like Uncle Ray and Uncle Reg and Auntie Audrey, and the Jenkins and Russells and Saiches.

Fortunately, Dad had negotiated that I could stay at Hitchin Boys' Grammar, though, technically, as we were moving to a different county – Bedfordshire – and out of Hertfordshire, I should have been transferred. This was some relief as Hitchin was at least friendly territory. My commute, however, along with my sister, would turn into a thirty-minute bus ride and involve a much earlier start in the morning.

If this move proved challenging for the children, it was little short of traumatic for my father. He had never imagined leaving his beloved St Ippolyts. It was where his family had found refuge and security in the uncertain decade of the 1930s. Here he had prospered, found confidence, friends and status. Everyone new Frank Wingate, Hitchin Town's star centre forward. Now we were going to an alien village where no-one had heard of him or us. Where we would be anonymous strangers, regarded by the locals as outsiders, interlopers.

Dad had developed a successful career at the Prudential Company, selling domestic and life insurances. He didn't particularly enjoy it, but tolerated it for the reasonable salary and independence it gave him. In fact, he was successful enough to have been offered promotion on several occasions. Instead of being on the lowest rank, as an agent, he could have become a District Superintendent, managing a group of agents. Had he been more ambitious he could then have become a District Manager and sat in a grand office, like his manager in Hitchin.

But Dad had turned down all offers in the past, for the simple reason that they would have meant leaving his village, and probably moving far and wide.

In 1961 circumstances had changed, however. With the arrival of Sally-Ann, two growing teenagers and Geoff already seven years old, we were running out of space. On top of this, Dad recognised that if he refused any more opportunities of advancement, he would have lost the possibility of future advancement.

He wasn't going to get a better offer than having to move only eight miles away, and so he accepted with a heavy heart. However, he made it very clear that he would not settle in the new place, but maintain all possible contact with St Ippolyts, down to meeting his regular drinking and cribbage mates at the Redcoats Pub on a Tuesday night. He was not going to acclimatise to a county which comprised of "Brussels sprout and potato fields" as opposed to the pasture lands of the green and wooded Chiltern Hills.

Such prejudices didn't exactly smooth the mental transition my mother and us children had to make. But there were advantages. Our new house, which my father was buying, was a new-built semi-detached. It lay across the road from an extensive park, on which, importantly, was the village football pitch. The house boasted central heating and a garage and its own telephone. The Wingates were definitely moving up in the world.

Nevertheless, this didn't make the prospect of the departure, set for the next spring, any easier to bear. To deal with the wrench from the only world I knew, was alarming. It marked the end of childhood and the beginning of adolescence, along with the increasing acceptance of responsibility and challenge. It signalled the end of a period of innocence, an acceleration of the process of growing up.

At the same time the world was changing and pushed into my consciousness. President Kennedy was sending soldiers to a far-off country in Asia, called Vietnam. And at the very end of that transformational year, they talked about a birth pill for women.

I really couldn't quite believe that we would be leaving our village behind. Our village with the strange name, the village of the patron saint of horses, which had nurtured me and prepared me for the world. It was time to say goodbye to familiar surroundings and venture out to face new experiences, people and places.

Chapter Eighteen
Exile

Before we settled into the village of Henlow in Bedfordshire, we imagined turning up like forlorn immigrants, bereft of friends and disoriented in an alien environment. It was hardly like that. Our new home wouldn't have won the Most Beautiful Village in England Award, or even in Bedfordshire, but it was a relaxed and welcoming place.

Henlow was a ribbon village stretching along the main Hitchin-Biggleswade Road, connecting those two market towns. It boasted nothing of special architectural or scenic value and was not distinguished in any particular way. Although the home of five pubs, for a population of perhaps five hundred, they were establishments rarely occupied by more than a handful of elderly male drinkers and aspiring under-age boozers. The Crown, however, on the crossroads and the nearest Henlow Camp, did become chock-a-block with tipsy couples at Christmas time.

Perhaps its greatest claim to fame was the nearby RAF base and aerodrome, which at least added an element of glamour for a twelve-year-old. But it also offered what was reportedly the UK's first "Beauty Farm". Called Henlow Grange, this establishment was situated discreetly a mile outside the village, away from the prying eyes of the locals, where celebrities and starlets, the famous and fortunate, escaped the public eye to remove wrinkles, restore energy and recapture their youth. Why, even Shirley Bassey and Jimmy Savile stayed there, so the place exuded an aura of mystique and untouchable glamour.

It was staffed by a team of live-in, sophisticated, heavily made-up young women, who were the object of intense interest to the testosterone-powered village lads. The potential Casanovas were, however, kept at arms' length by an eight-foot-high brick wall and a fearsome owner/manageress, called Mrs Costigan, who enjoyed the reputation of a Rottweiler. This "farm" was the former local manor house, and had its origins in the 17th century.

This didn't interest me personally, only aged twelve when moving there, so much as the village sports field opposite our new home. Henlow's football pitch, cricket pitch and pavilion were as grand as any village and where I quickly made new friends. Just a few hundred yards along our lane was the village primary school, which younger brother Geoff and baby sister Sally would attend, and at the end of that same lane a substantial village church, which dated back to the 14th century.

As my father had repeatedly and derogatively pointed out, the village was indeed surrounded by vegetable fields. Potatoes, Brussels sprouts and cabbages prospered in Bedfordshire's clay soil. Nevertheless, the absence of green fields around me was not a major problem, for soon, at the onset of puberty and teenage life, war games, building camps and roaming the countryside were, as pastimes, yielding to more attractive pursuits, such as youth clubs, discos, smoking and girls.

Being only six miles from the centre of my emerging social life, Hitchin, Henlow didn't seem too cut off, and even offered some distractions of its own.

Our new residence, in the centre of the village, was a marked improvement on our former council house. It was a newly built semi-detached, in a row of four doubles. Boasting a gas fire in the lounge its own telephone, a proper washing machine, a garage and small front and rear garden, it was modernity exemplified. Always overheated to the point of soporific semi-consciousness, it provided a domestic living experience like being smothered in warm cotton wool – a welcome contrast to the spartan conditions of earlier days.

With three bedrooms and a bathroom upstairs, lounge, dining room, kitchen, hallway and toilet downstairs, it was much larger than our former home. I shared one bedroom with my brother Geoff, sleeping in bunk beds, while sister Sue had her own room and baby Sally continued to sleep in my parents' bedroom.

Being a lot lighter and brighter, however, with larger windows, the house felt more spacious. The lounge and dining room were separated by a folding wooden partition, which was invariably left open. Because of the clutter of furniture in both lounge and dining room, these areas always seemed crowded but cosy.

Dad had insisted on buying a bulky, old-fashioned dining room set. Made of stained oak and dark green drapery, the chunky table, four chairs and sideboard virtually filled the entire dining room, so that manoeuvring around them was tricky. Meanwhile, the moderate sized lounge was soon overwhelmed with a new, large-screen colour TV, sofa set, armchairs, side tables, coffee table and – teenage delight – a record player!

Situated in the elegantly named Park Lane, this sophisticated home faced immediately opposite the rear of the cricket pavilion, which represented a potential hazard. We lived in fear in the summer of a cricket ball crashing through our front window! It never happened, though one or two did reach our front garden. My sister and I spent many a lazy, warm summer's afternoon lying on the grass, half studying, half watching the cricket.

Neighbouring our new home to the left side was a forbidding building known as "The Maltings", which was concealed behind a high fence. I never did enter it, nor discover what actually happened there. Presumably it was where barley or other grain was laid out to dry and germinate to create the malt that went into beer making.

The result for us next door was a pervasive, sweet, musty smell, particularly strong in the summer, which I'll always associate with that home.

Any trauma I suffered from leaving St Ippolyts soon evaporated. I had adapted to the grammar school in Hitchin without problem. Being a conscientious and deferential student I soon established myself academically, and I found I was good enough at rugby to make the school team and therefore enjoy the status of being one of the "in-crowd". The commute to school from Henlow was tiring sometimes, especially in the cold of winter, when early starts meant departing in the dark, and at weekends for school sports, but it proved tolerable. Off we would go the bus stop, my sister and I, her much taller than me, both laden with full satchels and duffel bags stuffed with sports gear.

More importantly, I soon made new friends in Henlow. My teenage years following the move were full of companionship and socialising. Puberty was a happy time of discovery and adventure. At first my group of friends centred around the Church and Youth Club, both of which were within ten minutes' walk of home. It was the most religious period of my life, when I attended Church on a Sunday quite regularly for about a year and was confirmed at fourteen. After that my interest in religion waned, however, as my curiosity focused on the Youth Club and particularly on the opposite sex populating it.

At this time, in my early teens, I also got a job, with my sister Sue. We somehow had ourselves hired as dishwashers at the glamorous Henlow Grange. Each Sunday morning we would stand before large, steaming sinks, sleeves rolled up, cleaning dozens of greasy plates, pots and pans. Our overseer was a jolly, overweight chef, a garrulous Russian, who was a good deal more interested in me than in my sister.

He took delight in teaching us how to stack and wash the cutlery, crockery, pots and pans in the correct order. "Sergei Stranovitch is my name", he intoned. "Sergei Organisation Obrunsky Stranovitch, because I am Organisation," he cackled, while insisting on popping chocolates into my mouth. I was well aware what was behind this attention, but it didn't worry me as he seemed harmless enough. His advances never went beyond the amusing, and sister Sue was there to keep an eye on things.

When I reached fifteen, social life took on a different dimension, with the arrival of new neighbours in the adjacent semi. Of the family of five, who came from Newcastle, one was a lad my age. With a mop of fair hair, cut in the fashionable Beatles style, a cheeky wit and a passion for football, Dave would become a "best mate" for those teenage years.

Whilst I was the steady school student, somehow fitting the study of History, Latin and other subjects, into an increasingly busy social diary, Dave eschewed all formal learning. He simply hated school and left as soon as he could, without acquiring any qualifications. Naturally bright and articulate he was quite determined to become a successful entrepreneur. Ideas of how to make a million fermented in his brain with frequent regularity.

Despite our superficial differences, we became firm allies in the pubescent search for sexual glory – largely unsuccessful but highly optimistic in its pursuit. Adopting the '60s trends of the day, we declared ourselves Mods – as opposed to greasy and aggressive Rockers – and set about styling ourselves as the fashion icons of the village.

Our cause was greatly enhanced when I reached sixteen, for I then acquired a motor scooter. That meant mobility and the geographic enlargement of our area of potential conquest. My second hand Vespa Sportique, which I crudely hand-painted in Luftwaffe camouflage, was the key to our ambition. The silencer was illegally punctured with hammer and nail, so that it would roar the more impressively around the lanes and byways of Bedfordshire and Hertfordshire.

There we were. Dave, the pillion passenger, dressed in ankle length red leather overcoat a la Rod Stewart, and a German army helmet for safety. Me, clad in three-quarter length black parka, with union jack sown on the back, revving up the 150 cc machine as impressively as possible. Image was all-important as we embraced the prevailing "mod" fashions of the day. In my Saturday night finest I might be clad in my green hipster trousers, my black-and-white check shirt and purple suede shoes.

How we impressed the girls of the local villages as we cruised through Shefford, Langley, Pirton, Arlesey and others on the Vespa. We dazzled them all! Or so we thought. What the girls concluded as we whizzed by, whooping and whistling, is probably best left unexplored.

At seventeen our social reach extended even further, as Dave and I befriended two other village boys. Graham and Brian (always known as Fuzz) were a year or two older than us and both possessed cars. Why Brian was called Fuzz seemed to be a mystery to all. Something to do with his hair perhaps. Generous to a fault, these two ferried us around, from pub to disco to party to day trip. Social life was quite a whirl as the Henlow "Gang of Four" explored the teenage fleshpots of North Hertfordshire and South Bedfordshire.

Fuzz's mother labelled us the "Four Naughty Boys of Henlow", but in reality the worst of our sins was probably getting home after midnight too often. We certainly drank too much beer, but never bothered with drugs and although we may have broken a female heart or two, we never knowingly broke the law. Nor did we get involved in the frequent Saturday night punch ups, being far too sophisticated for that kind of crude behaviour, or so we reasoned, though simple cowardice played its part too.

They were truly exciting times, coinciding with the outpouring of original music and fashion epitomising the Swinging Sixties. Our temples of worship were places such as the Hermitage Ballroom in Hitchin, the Mecca in Stevenage, the California Ballroom in Dunstable, as well as dance halls and discos in Luton, Letchworth and Biggleswade. We saw artists setting out in our local haunts that were to become global stars, such as the Cream, PJ Proby, Geno Washington and the Ram Jam Band, the Four Tops and many others. Here we strutted our stuff and attempted the latest dance steps in the effort to impress the girls.

These excursions were always fuelled by the consumption of plentiful supplies of beer – rarely anything stronger. It was just the convention for boys our age to drink pints of beer when socialising. On a regular Saturday night it was quite normal to swallow eight pints or so, between the restrictive hours of those days – that is between eight o-clock when we arrived at the pub or disco, and ten thirty when last orders were called.

At one period, when I was seventeen, still under age in theory, the gang or four developed the habit of attending Baldock Working Men's Club on a Sunday lunch time. We would head there in Graham's Triumph Herald, to arrive for twelve noon. The place would be packed with working men, their wives, their sons and daughters, and event their parents. A dense atmosphere of cigarette smoke, beer, chat, laughter and blue humour was quickly cooked up in the hall-like club. On stage a blue comedian, who, when not being shouted down, told crude jokes which set the assembled crowd cackling and guffawing. Meanwhile, the beer flowed. In between searching out the best looking girls our age and summoning up enough courage to talk to them, we slurped our pints. Four or five would be dispatched before it was time to head home for Sunday lunch. Either I managed to conceal the fact I was half inebriated or my parents chose to ignore it, but this practice never seemed to cause much comment from my parents!

This team of rural fashionados expanded our horizons as time went by. One summer we ventured to Devon on holiday together, staying for a week in a chalet on the beach at Dawlish. Domestically it was disorganised, but we had fun in the traditional British teenager way. We got sunburnt on the first day, so that our backs were red and raw for most of the week. We drank scrumpy to excess and became ill from it. We also went to local pubs and dance halls where we met exotic girls from Birmingham and Manchester.

The following year we smashed all social boundaries by flying on a package holiday to Rimini in Italy. I was so nervous of flying for the first time that I felt sick on take-off. I had to endure the indignity of being taken by an air hostess to lie down on the back row, while she bathed my brow with a cold towel. I was paralysed with humiliation, but my friends found the episode highly amusing.

In Rimini we holidayed again in the traditional way. We got sunburnt on the first day, became hungover from quaffing too much Asti Spumante, and went to local discos where we met exotic girls from Birmingham and Manchester.

Although the lifestyle was superficial and hedonistic, this group of friends still managed to maintain their work and study throughout. The others were hard workers and were building successful careers in construction, the motor trade and business. I did enough study to prepare myself for sixth form and then university. The day was looming when I would be eighteen and leaving home.

For me the transition from St Ippolyts to exile was painless, as the helter skelter of school and social life of my teenage years rapidly extinguished any lingering nostalgia. For my siblings and parents the transition wasn't so easy, however.

For sister Sue, two years older than me, and fourteen when we moved, the problem was my father. For whilst he gave me every loose rein to socialise as I wished, he attempted to protect the virtue of my sister by controlling her movements and setting deadlines for her coming home.

209

Neither did he approve of her having boyfriends, particularly boys from Henlow, whom he considered unworthy of his daughter.

Nevertheless, Sue was as strong-willed as him and the result was a confrontational relationship. Even then it had its ludicrous moments. She would meet one boyfriend in the cricket pavilion opposite our house, as she certainly wouldn't want to introduce him at home. At one time she met her local boyfriend Lionel almost every night in that romantic venue. Consequently, I had to act sometimes as lookout and give warning if Dad threatened to emerge from home to go looking for Sue.

The situation reached its apogee when Sue started at university. By then she was a confirmed radical and hippy, which alienated her further from Dad. Her boyfriend at that time, whose luxuriant red hair spilled down over his shoulders, came to Henlow to visit her one summer vacation. As he was not allowed near the house he spent an uncomfortable week squatting in the cricket pavilion across the lane. Mum was in on the subterfuge and food and provisions were duly smuggled over the road to the outcast suitor, who was in a pretty dishevelled state by the end of his ordeal.

Sister Sue took all this in her stride. She never missed St Ippolyts, and readily integrated into our new village, making friends and attracting boyfriends. Her intellect and her imagination were, however, already summoning her to more inspiring attractions than rural Bedfordshire or Hertfordshire could offer.

In general, we were well-behaved teenagers, but on one occasion we did disappoint our parents. Very unusually they decided to take a weekend away, taking the younger ones, Sally and Geoff, with them. Naturally, we faithfully promised to take good care of the house and not use it for any unauthorised activity. The next instant we were planning a party. At that time Sue was eighteen years old and I was sixteen.

We invited about twenty friends and planned the whole venture meticulously, so that there would be no evidence of untoward behaviour. We bought plastic cups and plates, so that nothing would be broken. To avoid possible damage, the living room furniture, including the TV and sofa, were carried upstairs on the morning of the event, as the living room was to become the disco dance area!

It was a relatively civilized affair. Despite quantities of beer and cider consumed, along with potato chips and other delicacies, and much dancing and snogging, everyone behaved reasonably. No obvious damage was caused and we had all day Sunday to clear up any festive traces and clean the place. The only slight problem was that an inch-long chip of wood was knocked from the TV housing as we carried it back downstairs. No problem, we thought, and simply glued it back into place.

Our returning parents were consequently greeted with blasé self-confidence, as we felt sure that our deceit was well concealed. Unfortunately, they discovered the truth within about five minutes. First, they immediately noticed that pieces of furniture were not quite in the right place. They spotted crumbs and debris under the sofa. Mum then returned from putting something into the dustbin, to ask us why there were thirty or so plastic cups and plates, along with empty beer and cider bottles in the bin. At that point, as we stood embarrassed in the living room, the chip of wood fell off the TV frame.

Our efforts at deception were found to be wanting and our feeling of guilt palpable enough. Our parents were

211

remarkably understanding and their expression of disappointment in our failure to live up to their trust was sufficient scolding. They never went away again leaving us at home and that remained the only teenage party we had.

For younger brother Geoff, the Henlow years were not especially enjoyable, as he had to deal with a lot of disruption. First, being only eight when we moved, he had to adapt to an entirely new primary school. As soon as he settled there, however, he had to move on to secondary school and the obvious destination was the grammar school in Biggleswade, the centre of the educational catchment area in which Henlow lay. The only problem was that my father insisted that he attend Hitchin Boys' Grammar School, partly because he regarded it as superior, but mainly because Hitchin was "home" and Biggleswade was foreign territory.

Consequently, my bemused brother, having spent just two years at the Stratton school in Biggleswade, and having made several good friends, was wrenched from that familiar environment and packed off to the Boys' Grammar in Hitchin. This was tough for him, as he had to make a clean start, without even the advantage of sharing any primary experiences or acquaintances. Needless to say, it was an unhappy transition period for him.

For the smallest one, Sally, who was only two when we moved, the family changes meant little, but for Geoff these years were unsettling.

But if Geoff found life insecure through these years, my mother found it mostly miserable. Leaving the small network of friends she had established in St Ippolyts over the years, she landed in the new situation without contacts. As a housewife she rarely ventured out, and apart from the daily local shopping trips, some minor chores and matters, such as visiting the hair stylist, and occasional weekends travelling to Hitchin, she remained largely isolated.

Two factors compounded her feeling of estrangement. One was her natural lack of public self-confidence. The other was my father's derisory view of her attempts to construct any social life for herself in Henlow, when she did have the opportunity.

She was an intelligent woman, but probably because she lost her father so young and was committed to a dull boarding school, she suffered from an underlying sense of insecurity. Living in daily danger in the war years in South London could only have compounded this. As a result, she was reluctant to engage in any public activity and was intensely private and domestic, which was normal enough for a housewife of her generation.

So she would never consider joining any clubs or choirs, or courses, for example. She never learnt to drive. She never developed any hobbies, or even read much. Our house was devoid of any serious literature – until my sister brought books home from university. This reticence was not so much a problem of personal shyness. On the contrary she was very gregarious and vivacious in company and popular. But she was passive and lacked any spirit of risk or adventure. Nothing would be attempted beyond her domestic or family comfort zone.

The new state of exile exacerbated her sense of alienation. She did make several friends, whom she retained – a neighbour and the lady in the village who regularly cut her hair. She would meet with them on occasion for coffee and gossip. Even these minimal relationships, however, were scoffed at by my father. What possible interest could these simple people have for her?

He wondered why she would bother when we certainly weren't going to settle in Henlow for long.

I noticed at the time, with a degree of irritation, that she took every opportunity to spend time with me and my friends when we were at home. This even meant she waited up until late, sometimes past midnight, to see if I had brought friends back for a last coffee. She would then sit with us, chatting and mildly flirting with the others. It was flattering to know that your mates considered your mother to be so hospitable and friendly, but it irked me that it inhibited our behaviour.

At that time, I thought this behaviour inconvenient. In retrospect it was the sign of a lonely person, seeking some companionship and fun. She was, in a sense, living life vicariously, as she had little socialising of her own to enjoy.

My father didn't appear to notice this. He had a very traditional view of a mother's role, typical of his generation. A mother stayed at home, looked after the household and children and supported her husband in his efforts to provide financial security. It was an important and satisfying role... wasn't it? He never recognised a growing sense of redundancy felt by my mother, especially as we children grew up and became less dependent on her. This lack of self-esteem was to lead to serious depression in later years.

Meanwhile, my father was leading a busy working and social life. He was industrious and conscientious at a job that nevertheless gave him little satisfaction or enjoyment. However, it was well paid and he was successful at it. Selling insurance in those days was a very personal, face-to-face, affair. The "Man from the Pru" (Prudential Insurance Company) knocked on your door; and like a vacuum cleaner salesman, won your acceptance through his presentable looks, charm and persuasive manner. Once you had invited him in, he became your friend, and readily advised you that you required not only life insurance, but several other policies, to make your family secure for the future. Having established the relationship, he then popped round every week to collect the premiums – which were so reasonable – in cash. He almost became part of the family.

Dad was good at this. He was presentable and affable. He got on well with people. His "patch" as a Section Superintendent, covered a wide rural area of South Bedfordshire, including the market town of Biggleswade and many ancient villages with names that echoed from the time of the Domesday Book – Gamlingay, Potton, Higham Gobion, Clophill, Shillington and many others. Covering such an area required a lot of driving and he worked most evenings, making his sales and collections.

In addition to collecting premiums, he enjoyed a lively social life. He related well with his six or so "agents" who reported to him, each covering their own geographic area. Many evenings, I suspect, when the premiums were secure, he enjoyed a pint or two at some pub or other, before coming home. These men, familiar to us, became good friends, with whom he played tennis, or went to watch Luton Town play. Unlike my mother, he was enjoying some gaiety, good humour and companionship.

At the same time, he studiously avoided any social interaction in Henlow, uninterested in forming any relationship with the place or its people. He was never unfriendly or discourteous with anyone, just detached and indifferent. For him, this phase of life was an exile, and a temporary one at that.

He carefully maintained his links with St Ippolyts by driving over there each Tuesday night and Sunday lunch time to meet his cronies. With the same, unchanging set of two or three old friends he would play cribbage and sip a beer or two.

For me, however, he remained the perfect father. As the eldest son, able at sport and capable as a student, I was the apple of his eye. During my teenage years he gave me all practical support, ferrying me to my rugby and soccer matches, cheering me on, picking me up at inconvenient times and places. He was always there. He wasn't demonstrably affectionate, but his love was obvious.

It was not necessarily so for the others. He was kind with his children, but his relationship with sister Sue became stormier, as she grew more independent minded and argumentative. It was a relief for both of them when she left to go to university. Similarly, he was never harsh with the two younger ones, but largely uncomprehending of Geoff's artistic talents, of which he had no appreciation. Loving enough to little Sally, he didn't have so much time to spend with her.

Exile made him more detached from his home and family. He felt uprooted and homesick, with no emotional ties to his house and homestead. Going home to Henlow was not going home. In those years, being entirely selfishly preoccupied with my own friends, studies, sports and girlfriends, I still considered my family life to be a model of harmony and inspiration. As I look back I recognise the fault lines developing between children and parents and between parents. Between my mother and father, the affection was ebbing away.

Then, quite suddenly, in 1968, just as the Western world was rocked with anti-Vietnam demonstrations in the US, revolution in the streets of Paris, and student tumult in the UK, Dad dropped a bombshell. He had achieved a transfer back to the Hitchin district. The exile was coming to an end and he was determined to find a home in his beloved St Ippolyts.

Family reactions were mixed. Sue didn't really care. She was already studying Philosophy and English at Nottingham University and leading the unconventional lifestyle that was to mark her next years. She wouldn't really return home for a decade. Geoff, then fourteen, had already undergone the wrench of changing to the Boys' Grammar in Hitchin and would find living closer to that town more convenient.

For Mum, I think she accepted the move with weary resignation. She would be closer to a few old friends St Ippolyts way, but she would lose those she had made in Henlow. Dad made the decisions, anyway.

For myself, the move coincided with preparations to go to university, so took a secondary priority in my thinking. I would soon be leaving home, so it wouldn't make much difference to me. I was certainly going to miss the close ties with the Gang of Four, but also had many friends in Hitchin, where social life was centred.

Dad searched for a new home in St Ippolyts. His solution was satisfactory, but, ironically, failed in its main objective. The new-built house he finally purchased was about ten yards short of his dream. Lying on a quaint, narrow lane on the fringes of the town of Hitchin, it was firmly situated in the parish of Hitchin, whereas the boundary of the parish of St Ippolyts ran down the centre of the lane. We came within spitting distance of returning. No matter, my father was content. The exile had come to an end.

Our new home was slightly larger than the previous one, detached and private. It was comfortable and light but without character. It lay on the edge of a new estate of thirty or forty houses, about two miles from Hitchin town centre. I was to live there for about six months in 1969, from the time we moved in until the day I started nervously at Oxford University.

I didn't share my father's longing for St Ippolyts, nor his affection for the village, at that time. With all the overweening assuredness of an eighteen-year-old self-declared intellectual and radical reformer, I viewed St Ippolyts, and indeed Hitchin, as irrelevant. I had outgrown them and anticipated conquering vibrant cities and far-flung exotic locations. Most friends had by this time moved on, so there was little reason even to visit the village with the strange name.

Life soon took me away to university, afterwards to Yorkshire and eventually to the other side of the world, to Hong Kong. There was initially small reason to think of my original home. But as years passed in my Hong Kong career, it became increasingly important to return to the family home in Hitchin, where my mother and father were quietly living out their years. I wanted to see them and the rest of the family, and the distance away and foreign nature of life abroad gave the familiar surroundings new allure. They offered calm and security, re-assurance, when everyday life in Asia was hectic, exciting and draining.

I also developed renewed curiosity about St Ippolyts, often, on my holidays, walking or jogging around those country lanes.

Much remained unchanged. In general I found it unremarkable. There were one or two new housing developments, one of which covered over the orchard at the bottom of the rec where we had once stolen apples. The sights and sounds of my early youth were still present, but less colourful, drab even, and the village seemed worn. Our family council house was much the same. I noticed that the recreation ground was shabby, with weeds growing through the asphalt. The nearby allotments, that had once been so orderly and carefully manicured by their owners, lay mostly neglected.

Even the smell of the place had become more anodyne. No acrid whiff of burning coal, or freshly mown grass, or even the lingering odour of manure from the fields. But perhaps the perceived mediocrity was just the result of a person getting older, pointlessly trying to recapture sensations that were no longer to be experienced.

Despite sensory disappointments, these visits were comforting and interesting. The location inspired the memory to drag up ghosts from the past. The Jenkins family, Mr Livingstone the teacher, Philip Coutts, Hans the German, Horace the road sweeper and Alfie Turner. All characters in a background that helped shape my principles and prejudices; that gave me a foundation on which to grow.

My short time there, my first decade, can be seen as a typical microcosm of British society in the 1950s, emerging from the harrowing years of war and consequent austerity. It was also a momentary episode in the continuing story of a country village with a history stretching back over a thousand years.

The End